ISBN: 978-0-9837161-9-8

Other Books by Afdhere Jama:

At Noonday with the Gods of Somalia

Illegal Citizens

Queer Jihad

Naked Trees

Being Queer and Somali

*To all the young people who
grow up thinking they are alone.*

Acknowledgements

I want to acknowledge that none of this would be happening if it weren't for my mother. My mother raised me with love and instilled in me the idea of being proud of who and what I am. She *saw* me, she knew me, and she really loved me. So, thank you very much, Mom.

If the stories in this book had taught me anything it is that family love really makes a big difference. We are all truly a sum of our experiences, and if those experiences, especially the ones from the early part of life, if those experiences are not positive then life will not be so positive.

I would like to acknowledge my sister in the struggle, Hadiyo Jim'ale, who has been very supportive through all of my work, but who has been extremely helpful in the gathering of this book.

I would like to acknowledge all of the subjects in this book. Thank you for entrusting me with your stories, for taking me into your lives, and thank you so much for being part of this historic book!

Thank you to all the people who supported this book in the various stages of its birthing. Some of these people I would like to thank directly:

I thank Sharifa Ismail for the love, emotional support, and for financing some of the projects herself. Thank you for helping me pay for my trip to meet Hamdi, my first Somali subject. Thank you so much!

I want to thank Jennifer Ahmed, who was always my lifeline and slept with her cellphone under her pillow just in case something happened to me while I was wherever I happened to be. I know all the things you have done for me, Jennifer, and I sincerely thank you—I will never be able to repay you!

Abu Omar, my dear friend and colleague who never let me forget why I was doing what I was doing whenever I would get discouraged by all the horrible things that happen in the world; he supported me always professionally as well by single-handedly taking over *Huriyah* whenever I needed him to. I would be lost without you. Thank you for everything.

Leila Hosseini—my Persian superwoman whom I had the pleasure of enjoying her very much human abilities of unconditional love, dedication, and support. They say people come into your life for a reason. Thank you!

Also, Daayiee Abdullah—for your friendship, encouragement and counsel. It wouldn't have been the same without you. Thank you!

Last but not least Rahal Eks—you're my soul buddy. I'm thankful for all the things we are doing, all the wonderful experiences and all that is yet to come. Thank you!

Introduction

Being queer and Somali is being part of two "different" groups. In the queer American community I'm different because I'm Somali; and in the Somali community I'm different because I'm queer. I consider myself to be of many things, I especially consider myself to be a global person. I have said to many people; that being global is the only way I know to juggle my many identities.

The truth of the matter is that being Somali is not just based on what I say, it is also what others say. It is not just my life, but also the lives of others. Despite our common connections, and there are many connections Somalis have, not all Somalis see the world through the same lenses. I learned that through telling the stories of queer people in the Somali community.

Hamdi Suldan was my first queer Somali subject, and after hundreds and hundreds of other subjects in the years I have been writing about LGBT life in the Somali community, I had learned a few things. These things would help me over the years to be get strong in my own personal journey, as the stories of these people showed me that I was indeed *worthy* of what I believed.

The first thing I learned was that there are a lot of queer Somalis who are in relationships they had not chosen for themselves. I met so many gay men and women who were in marriages arranged by their families. Over and over again that was a theme that kept showing up in these stories, some escaping it by running away from home and others disowned by their families.

"Sunni Muslims believe that marriage is half of your faith," says Hadiyo Jim'ale, leader of the Queer Somalis organization. "Part of it has to do with tribalism, as that is another added pressure. Many Somalis are expected to marry members of their own tribe."

My family has many issues, and trust when I tell you that I'm the first to say they are not perfect at all, but I never felt pressured to marry let alone be forced to marry someone. Neither was my brother, nor my sisters. My family just doesn't do that.

The second thing I learned was that a lot of queer Somalis have had negative experiences associated with their sexuality from family, friends, and the larger Somali community. I met many people whose families disowned them, or whose families have been very negative towards them, or whose families have impacted them negatively by the way they spoke of queer sexuality.

I grew up in a family where I heard my mother defend me as a child many times. There is a clear conversation that comes to my mind, and it is a conversation that has given me so much strength. I must have been seven or eight, something like that, when I overheard a conversation between my mother and older sister. My sister suggested that I was going to grow up being a homosexual, and my mother said that she loves me nevertheless. I knew the word *qaniis* meant something unkind, as it was a word used by kids to refer to each other as a weapon, but I don't think my friends or I ever knew what it really meant.

I have never, ever, not even once heard negative thing being said about queer sexuality in a religious way. Everything I heard about *qaniisiinta*, or homosexuals, was cultural related. That is, I did not grow up with a negative idea of being queer. I would go to the mosque often and never did I hear a Friday Prayer focus on that subject. That is perhaps I grew up in a time in Somalia when salafism had not taken root just yet, when music and dance was part of Islam and the Sufi Tradition had a big influence in society.

I heard about the story of Lut, but it was never a focus and no one really ever explained what and who those people were. They sounded like a bunch of criminals from what I gathered.

Therefore, I did not grow up with a negative association between my sexuality and my culture.

Did you notice how seamlessly I interwoven the Muslim part of the Somali into the story? I took the story of Lut, associations, and culture.

That brings me to the queer side of this book. The queer side of this book is just as personal as the Somali side of this book. There are ethnic groups in some parts of the Muslim World who do not have to deal with the negative ideologies of being queer.

It wasn't until I was in my late teens that I realized just because I didn't have any issues with my sexuality it didn't mean others didn't. When I was a teenager I met and fell in love with one Somali guy. Like me he had no problems with what we were doing. We were doing it secretly, just as a man and a woman were doing it secretly. The issue was that we were having sexual relationship, not that we were having homosexual sexual relationship.

Later that year I went to the United States and I again met and fell in love with another guy. I know, I know, I easily fell in love. This second man, who grew up in a semi-religious household, had issues with it. He would feel bad after we had sex, and one time even commented how he had hoped we would change.

You could say it was the first time I realized there was an issue with people about their sexuality, which of course made me want to understand the issue better.

This experience led me to question whether it really was the case that Islam sees sexual relationship between people of the same sex as negative, or if it was cultural situation. Ultimately I came to the understanding that it was indeed cultural, and that different Muslim cultures approached this differently. The cultural approach was, in my new-found understanding, the same way different schools of thought approached this issue differently.

My books about sexuality are, I would argue, my experiences of coming to that understanding. It was only natural that I had started with my community, the first story I ever wrote being that of a Somali transgendered woman, but it was not long before I was onto the larger Muslim community. It was how the book *Illegal Citizens* came about. That book was about the everyday LGBT people living in Muslim communities in the Global South. Most of the people in that book are not out.

Queer Jihad was about the people in the Muslim communities, especially those in the safety of western countries, who are leading the fight for non-heteronormative understanding of issues relating to sex and sexuality. With that book I interviewed people like the first openly gay imams, activists, artists, and people who are generally in the public eye. Most of the people in that book are out. *Queer Jihad* was the love song I would dedicate to a young Muslim anywhere who wonders if it is okay to be queer and Muslim. It answers that question from many different angles.

Being Queer and Somali, therefore, is only different from those books because it combines the everyday and the activists, and it focuses on just my own ethnic community or people whose ethnic backgrounds are in the Somali communities of the Horn of Africa. Most people in this book are not out, even though most of them are out of the Somali communities of Africa. If *Queer Jihad* was my love song to the queer Muslim, then *Being Queer and Somali* is my love song to the queer Somali.

Truly, I write these books as they come. As I heal I share the healing. Meeting all of these people in my books, both the Somali and non-Somali, has been extremely enriching to me. It has been enriching because ever since I was a teenager, ever since I had that encounter with that self-hating young man, I had been forced to deal with people who either were self-hating or ones who thought it was their divine duty to tell me to become a self-hating queer man. The subjects in this book had given me all the confidence because I had the privilege to hear over and over again how our lives are just natural, just like everyone else's.

I'm grateful that I have had the awesome privilege to grow up in my family. I'm grateful for having had the pleasure to meet all these wonderful queer Somalis, queer Muslims, and queer people of color through the years.

Those of you who are young and Somali, and especially those of you who are wondering if your natural feelings are unnatural, this book is for you.

Queer

Before I talk about being queer, I want to talk about what the word itself means to me. It s important for people to understand why I use this word, especially since many people still see it as a word that has a negative background.

What is queer? For me, queer is an inclusive word that is an umbrella for anyone and everyone outside the heteronormative equation. That is, anyone who has a "different" sexuality or gender identity, an identity which is not traditionally sanctioned or accepted by mainstream society.

In Somali we have a word similar to this word. As a kid I used to hear the phrase, "Qajac, qajac, Khadiijo Warsame!" I never knew exactly who Khadiijo Warsame was, but I definitely know what the *qajac* part meant. It meant weird, strange, and it was also a word used against feminine men or masculine women, men and women outside of heteronormative sexuality or gender identity.

Similarly, queer is a word that was once used by society to describe weirdness, strangeness, and it was also a word used against gay and lesbian people.

As such, I'm owning that history by using these terms in positive ways. I liken it to the way that young Black men in the United States use the word "nigga," to own and celebrate a word that has been used against Black people.

In Arabic, there were several words. That has to do with Arabic being the primary or secondary language of couple of a dozen people in the Arab World. Their diverse culture allows them to have access to different kinds of Arabic. For example, in the early 2000s, while living in San Francisco and a member of SWANABAQ (Southwest Asian & North African Bay Area Queers), a group as diverse as the Arab community at large, there was a need to come up with positive terminology for the LGBT community.

This discussion, which was led by Lebanese-born Bassam Kassab, ended with a list of couple of dozen positive words. These words included "mithli," which literally means "same" and was to be used for same-sex or gay. Then there was "ahrar el jins," which literally means "free sex/gender/sexuality" and was to be used as an umbrella word much like queer. The later one was purely knew, while the former was a compromise on what good scientists have used in the later part of the 20th Century, "junusiya mithliya" (people of same sexuality), much like "homosexuality".

In 2000, when a group of LGBT Somalis sat down to choose an umbrella word for a social group that was going to be created after that meeting, a fierce debate ended with us deciding on "Qajacyada Soomaaliyeed" or "Queer Somalis." It was the first time that the word was used positively in regards to LGBT persons.

The debate on "qajac" came out of the diversity of the group. Some of us were from Somalia (now divided into Somalia, Puntland, Khatumo State, and Somaliland), while others were from the Somali communities in Ethiopia, Kenya, and Djibouti. Much like the discussion that went on in the LGBT Arab community, we realized not all of us were comfortable with using existing words to describe our experience. That is, people were just not willing to use words that they had individual negative or positive experiences in different cultural understanding within the larger Somali community.

I will never forget the case Hadiyo Jim'ale made to a young man who cried at the thought of using such a word to describe people like him. She hugged him tightly and said, "Honey, that is exactly why we need to use this word. We need to turn it around so that its painful past helps us to become a more joyful community today. We need to acknowledge our painful past to live a joyful present."

Interestingly enough, there were the same kind of debates and discussions on the use of the word "queer" as a positive word in the English-speaking communities, too. In my own life, I have older friends who just couldn't bring themselves to accept the word as a positive word. On the other hand, I have younger friends for whom the word has no negative associations.

For me, as a teenager of the 1990s, the word is just powerful and inclusive. Yet, I realize it is a word, like many other words, that comes with its own baggage. What I love about the word the most, and I suspect it is the same for people like me who have associations of both camps, it reminds me the good and the ugly at the same time.

Being queer, therefore, in my opinion, is such a privilege. Maya Angelou, whose work and life I continue to celebrate, may she rest in peace, once said that when you know better you do better. Being queer gives me that privilege of knowing better.

I understand what it is to be the weird, strange, "other." I have taken that privilege all my life, wherever I was. I remember being a kid in Somalia and deeply feeling one with the Mushunguli people, a group of people who had been oppressed by Somali people who look like me. The Mushunguli people, also known as Somali Bantu, were brought to the Somali community as slaves during a period when parts of what are now Somalia, Kenya, and Tanzania were under the Sultanate of Oman.

I remember living in a refugee camp in Kenya, and sharing my small allowance with friends I knew did not have relatives in Europe or North America, the way I did, friends who did not get money through *xawala* or remittance on a monthly basis.

I remember being a new immigrant in the United States, and helping other Somalis who did not have as much success in the country, as I had come to the country with some basic understanding of the English language. I remember translating for them with my broken language, and I remember one afternoon a doctor looking at me and asking with his eyes, "How are you able to do this! You don't speak the language properly yourself!"

It was, of course, no surprise to me that I also became interested in telling the stories of queer people, especially queer Somalis, even though I didn't have the education necessary to do such a thing. I basically had to learn how to interview my subjects as I went. I remember interviewing Hamdi Suldan, the trans woman whose story appears in this book (see "Seattle"), and her helping me with the interview questions.

Privilege.

Does that mean I think being queer makes you automatically one who uses that knowledge, that privilege, to be better? Of course, not. I have faced racism and Islamophobia from some queers, especially after 9/11. I have seen some queer men act as sexist towards women, even to queer women, as much as some of the hetero dudes. I have seen the way some queer people have put transgender rights in the back burner, as if gender rights are not as important as the fight for sexuality rights. I have seen queer organizations get behind Islamophobic initiatives, or anti-Semitic sentiments, or racist propaganda.

Nevertheless, I believe that that knowledge, that privilege, is there.

That is what being queer means to me.

Somali

If you drank the cool-aid that to be Somali means you have one look, one religion, and one language, I'm here to tell you otherwise.

I belong to a group of Somalis who speak a language we call "Af Maxaa Tiri." It is true that those of us who natively speak this language do look similar, and predominantly share the same faith, and have the same language, of course. In terms of our looks, for example, we are Cushitic people and therefore look similar to other Cushitic peoples in other parts of Africa such as those in Ethiopia, Eritrea, Ethiopia, Sudan and Egypt.

It is also true that those of us of the "Af Maxaa Tiri" camp have had the privilege to dominate the cultural dialogue, both at home and at abroad. The majority of Somali entertainers, for example, are of this group. Popular Somali faces like supermodel Iman, author Nuruddin Farah, and actor Barkhad Abdi are all from this group.

It is also true that until 1991, when the government of Mohamed Siad Barre was ousted out of Mogadishu, that that camp had dominated the political spectrum as well. For example, all of the presidents in recent history have been the "Af Maxaa Tiri" people.

But we are not the only Somalis.

People will tell you that Af Maxaa Tiri and Af Maay Maay are the same language but different dialects.

That is not true.

The Waqooyi and Koonfur dialects are dialects of the

same language, both belonging to the Af Maxaa Tiri, but Af Maay Maay is a different language. I can understand the Waqooyi, or northern, dialect, even though I was raised in the south and speak the Koonfur dialect.

When I listen to Somali singer Daleys sing in Af Maay Maay, which she does beautifully, I don't understand much of it. Despite growing up just 250 kilometers, or 155 miles, away from Baidhabo, the largest city where Af Maay Maay is spoken widely, I don't understand it.

Of course, there are also other languages like Af Tuni, Af Reer Xamar, Af Mushunguli, Af Garre, Af Barawaani, Af Baajuun, and many others and none of which I understand fully. I say "fully" because I'm a product of Mogadishu in the 1980s, and therefore I grew up around children who spoke some of these languages. I grew up in a system where once in a great while you would hear on television a song, or perhaps watch a scene, or a small break from the mainstream language.

Now, let's talk about that "Somali" look. As far as I know, there are mainstream (and I say mainstream because we constitute the loudest and most oppressive) Somalis, who have Cushitic features and to which my family belongs. We tend to have dark skin, long necks, and slim bodies. Our faces might be round or long, our eyes are generally pronounced and our hair soft, and with narrow noses.

But there are also other Somalis like the Reer Xamar, who literally are as light skinned as you can imagine. One of them, a childhood neighbor whose name was Nahar, had green eyes and when we would play in the sun too long he would get these big burns, which made him the recipient of many nasty jokes. We used to call him "cadaawe" (white boy), which he really disliked very much.

Nahar's family had belonged to Mogadishu much longer than my own family did. We used to go to his grandfather's house, which was in the old town of Mogadishu, in the Xamar Weyne neighborhood, and he would ask Nahar to memorize the names of their forefathers. I remember being so impressed by these families and their longevity to the area, going back all the way to the 8th Century.

There are also the Mushunguli, or Somali Bantu, whose ancestors were enslaved out of other parts of Africa under the orders of the Sultanate of Oman. When they were freed by the Italian decrees of the early 1900s, their status might have changed legally but it didn't fair any better socially. They are to this day called "adoon" (literally, "slave"), which is ironic because the Gulf Arabs call us "'abd" (its equivalent in Arabic) as their drivers and maids.

One of the most painful memories of my childhood is the day I was eating with the children of our Mushunguli maid, Jiijo, and my aunt walked into the house and saw me. She slapped me, made me spit out the food in front of them, and warned me to "never eat with the adoon." She reminded me how not long ago our families owned theirs, and that they worked for us still and we would never be the same. I was deeply scarred by that experience.

It is indeed interesting how sometimes the universe teaches us lessons. The same aunt would call me one night many years later, complaining that her Arab employer in the Middle East had called her "slave" ('abd). It took everything in me not to say to her that Karma was for real.

There are also the Baajuun. They are literally the people who lived in the Swahili Coast in the heyday of the Omani Kingdom. When I was in Kismaayo, especially in the Calanleey neighborhood, I remember seeing those faces, the same faces I would later see in Mombasa and Zanzibar. Their *taraab*, which my family thought was weird, is the same kind of entertainment as you would find in the other areas of the Swahili Coast.

Being Somali to me, therefore, means being part of a diverse culture, with diverse languages and peoples. I grew up in Somalia, in my opinion, in the best of times.

I remember being a kid, and traveling with my friends from Baar Ubax to Liido Beach. I remember the wonderful groups of Somalis I would encounter there, the kids I would meet and the languages I would hear. These beaches were as diverse as the beaches of California, where in Venice Beach, for example, I would one day also encounter a whole lot of other people. Venice Beach reminded me so much of Liido. Like Liido it was a beach you could visit and you would wonder, "Are all of these people living here?"

I knew our culture was diverse because we ate foods from Ethiopia, West Africa, the Middle East, Mediterranean, Indian, and even Chinese. Canjeelo, the Somali injera, was just Somali to me. Kaare, the Somali curry, was Somali to me. Baasto, the Somali pasta, was Somali to me. Bilaawe, the Somali pilau, was Somali to me. Xalwad, the Somali halva, was also Somali to me.

That is because being Somali is not "one" thing. It has to do with our history, as our history is part of the history of the Ethiopians, several Arab peoples, Italians, French,

West Africans, Indians, and the many other influences that we don't even know about.

I grew up in a city that was literally called "The Seat of the Shah" (Muqdishah, or Muqdisho, or Mogadishu, or "maqad el shah" in Arabic). It was also informally, and especially by the "Af Maxaa Tiri" folks like my parents, called "Xamar" or "light skinned city" (remember the "Reer Xamar" from above?).

The Arabic language has been big part of my life. In fact, when I was born, there was a *wadaad*, a religious scholar, who came and recited verses of the Qur'an above me. My mother used to tell me this story, where I would watch this man and listen to him. I was born merely a few hours before, but he caught my attention. I guess because he was speaking a language I wasn't used to when I was hanging out in my mother's womb.

I grew up speaking the Arabic language, being taught to me first as a second language as a four year old in Qur'an school. That wasn't their intention, and you didn't learn the language if you weren't paying attention, which I can assure you most of my friends did not. But I was fascinated, and I loved the way the *tafseer*, the interpretation of the Qur'an for our times, was done by our *macalin* or teacher. "Alxamdu, mahad, lillaahi, ilaahey baa iskaleh, Maaliki, Boqorka, youm-il-diin, maalinta aakhiro...."—this mix of the two languages, it fascinated the heck out of me!

Later, as a six year old, in mainstream school, my Arabic continued in "Arabic and Religion" class, which in my opinion was just really an Arabic class, as we read everything in Arabic. At one point we had a teacher in third grade, and I knew better Arabic than he did, and he really didn't like that.

I also had cousins who spoke Arabic as a first language, because they grew up in Kaambo Carab, an entire complex of Arabs and had Arab nannies while their cosmopolitan parents studied in Moscow and Washington DC. I used to love visiting them and watching with them Arabic movies and "Iftah Ya Simsim," or the Arabic version of Sesame Street.

I grew up also being cursed in Italian when my mother was upset with me. "Faan kuulo" was a Somali phrase to me. It didn't occur to me at all that it was Italian, and certainly not any more than I thought baasto had its roots in Italy; even though I later thought the Italians were missing out by not eating their pasta with banana.

That said, we knew our connection to Italy. We learned the many *gabay*, male poetry, against them in school, and I heard the *buraanbur*, female poetry, against them at weddings. We had friends who were from Italian-mix background. My older sister was a big fan of Marisa Karbooni, who was an actress with Italian and Somali parents. I also knew about aunts who were maids in Italy, something they would never have done in Somalia; and because they sent money back home it was okay with everyone else, too. During the civil war, our dreams were not to make it to London or Paris but to Rome and Milan.

I think about the *xawaash*, the spices, and how they were just Somali to me. The fact that most of them were imported from India was news to me. The *dirac*, the sensual caftans the women in my family wore, was just Somali to me. The fact that it was *saari* material imported from India was news to me. And I loved Cali Dheere, the Somali name for Amita Bachchan, just like I loved Somali stars like Maxamed Saleebaan Tubeec, because Bollywood was so much part of our lives that many of us learned Hindi in the process, as there were no subtitles.

Similarly, the African influences were everywhere. I grew up with *cambuulo*, bean mix from Kenya, and it was something we had used in our celebration at each graduation from *jus* or Qur'anic portion. Our women used *baati*, which are Tanzanian garments, in a local way as *guntiino*, the beautiful way of draping the garment around the body and knotting it over the left shoulder. During the *instunka*, we celebrated the new harvest season; the same exact way people do in Mozambique, Zanzibar, and Mombasa, by beating ourselves with sticks.

So, the influences of African, Arab, Indian, and European were part of our lives. They were part of what made us Somali because we consumed them regularly in our daily lives throughout the year.

Does that mean a more indigenous Somali culture does not exist? Of course, there is a local culture. But you have to know that it varies also. The local culture in Berbera is very different from the local culture of Kismaayo, as Kismaayo is very different from that of Bosaaso, as Bosaaso is also very different from that of Garissa, and the culture of Garissa is very different from that of Jigjiga.

Many of us also don't like to talk about how religions influence our cultures, just as cultures influence the religions. If you look at Somalia alone through religious lenses, you will be amazed.

The indigenous religious culture of the Somali is also very diverse. To understand it better, one must better understand the tribal system. The Af Maxaa Tiri people of Somalia have, more or less, always been very much connected, even if many of them will refuse to admit this reality. You can find most of the main tribes in all the parts of the countries in an indigenous kind of way.

The Hawiye, for example, has varies parts of its clans in different parts of the countries. The Habar Gidir can claim nativity to Galgaduud, for example, while the Abgaal can claim nativity to Mogadishu area. The Gaaljecel can claim nativity to in and around Libooyo, in and out of the border with Kenya.

At the same time, Daarood clans also can claim nativity in varies parts. For example, the Majeerteen in and around Bosaaso, the Mareexaan in Gedo, or the Ogaden in Ethiopia's Somali region, as well as the Ogaden in the Somali region of Kenya.

Likewise, the Dir clan of Gudubuursi might claim nativity with the Isaaq clans in the north or Waqooyi, while the Dir clan of Biyomaal might claim nativity with the Gaaljecel in Kismaayo area.

At the same time, the Isaaq clans are generally in northwestern Somalia, but there are also Isaaq clans in Ogadenia, alongside the Daarood clans.

In other words, we, the Af Maxaa Tiri people, intermarry, we speak the same language, we fight often, and ultimately we end up in the same faiths, too.

Look at Waaq, for example, the pre-Islamic god of the Af Maxaa Tiri people.

The best place to start is Caabud Waaq. What is fascinating about Caabud Waaq is that its name is a combination of Arabic and pre-Islamic terminology, which shows you that it continues to exist as such, or continued as such recently, even if its people no longer recognize the rituals as worshipping a non-Islamic god. The word "caabud" comes from "holy service" in Arabic (the "c" in Somali is the Arabic "3ayn").

In the night, in and around Caabud Waaq, in the state of Galgaduud, especially during the dry season of jiilaal, women sing "na bibiyaay, bibiyaay, bibiyaay, bibiya!" If you ask them to tell you what they're doing, they have no idea. The fact that this is a pre-Islamic practice of praying to Waaq during the cooler evenings in the hot summer is lost on them. The phrase literally says, "give us water" in an older generation of the language (currently this would be "noo biyee" in the Somali usage of that area).

They will also have no way to explain what "bashbash iyo barwaaqo," a greeting used in many parts of Somalia, means. "Bashbash" literally mimics what it is to dance on the ground with rainwater: bash bash, bash bash. The second part of the phrase, "barwaaqo," literally says "Waaq's blessing." In other words, the greeting, which is used all year round, says, "I'm blessed by Waaq".

At the Somali-Kenya-Ethiopian border, in the Somali state of Gedo and the Kenyan district of Mandera, there is a town called Ceel Waaq or El Wak. It literally means "Well of Waaq," and it still remains a town where animals come from all over the area to drink, where people get their water, and where water is plentiful even when it is not elsewhere. The population in the area is still very much pastoralists, too.

Legend has it that the ancestors lived barbarically in Malao, in the Waqooyi or north, when a long and awful *abaar* or famine struck the community. They left the area and went south, hoping things would get better. By the time they reached the red lands, or Galgaduud, they began to pray to Waaq, acknowledging their badly lived lives and to atone for their sins.

"But the famine continued," my grandmother used to tell me.

They continued their journey even more south until they reached Gedo or the green valley. There the rains came, and they were able to finally nourish their bodies and their animals. They called the area the "Well of Waaq," and went back the way they came, although leaving some families behind, as they knew they might need to return again.

They stopped in Galgaduud again, and prayed once more and called the area "Caabud Waaq." Believing it was their prayers that gave them rains in the south, they began to establish roots there, too. They wanted to come back and make it a holy land, even though it was otherwise undesirable as a place to live (not very close to the commerce of the seas).

When they finally reached back home, they began using the word Barbara (barbaric period) to refer to land of their kingdom, as never to return to their previous unawareness, and today that is the official Somali name for Malao.

My grandfather used to tell me how all year long his family would travel in parts of what are now Somalia, Puntland, Somaliland, Djibouti, Ethiopia, and Kenya. Chances were if one area was having issues, whether it was war going or natural disasters taking place, another area was better off. At every stop, there were local people who spoke like them, and some were even related to them.

That is how all these clans from the same tribes ended up all over the place.

Now, if you look at the religious history of those outside of the Af Maxaa Tiri group, it gets even more interesting.

As such, being Somali is far more complicated than being queer. I became a refugee not because I'm queer but because I'm Somali. What hurts us Somalis is our denial of our histories, whether religious or linguistic or anything else, in an imagined honor of the tribe.

The sad thing about being Somali hit me hardest the first time I was in India. Here was a nation in which 80% of the country belongs to Hinduism, a religion in which there is as many gods as there are days in the year.

According to Gadadhara Pandit Dasa, a well-respected Hindu scholar in the United States, there are as many as 33 million Hindu gods. In an article for the Huffington Post, he explained that Hinduism understands it needs more than one authority to keep things going, as would any government.

Here was Somalia, a country that is predominately Muslim, and predominantly Sunni. Those of us who are responsible for the civil war also speak the same language, and generally look similar. We are the mainstream culture. So, exactly what are we fighting about?

Tribalism.

So, tribalism has hurt me more than homophobia. It hurts women more than sexism. It hurts our youth, our culture, and our faiths. Thanks to tribalism, terrorists like Osama bin Laden were able to come and invest their culture in our midst. Thanks to tribalism, our young are fighting in wars that are not theirs, in places like Syria and Iraq. Thanks to tribalism, our women are being hauled to court as funders of terrorism in places like London and Minneapolis.

As such, being a Somali means remembering that I come from a long history, a rich culture, and diverse background; that I have a beautiful language, and that whatever is wrong with my culture will one day find its solutions; and that I'm committed to be part of that solution.

Muslim

Being a Muslim, to me, is much more than just belonging to a particular faith. It is a way of life, it is being part of a larger culture, and it is also, yes, being part of a particular faith.

When I was born, my parents invited a local *wadaad*, or religious scholar, and he recited verses of the Qur'an over me. That was after he had sung the *adhan*, or call to prayer, into my ears.

A few days later, another man was invited. This one belonged to the Yibir tribe, which collects *samaanyo*, a gift paid to their tribe in exchange for their blessing newborns.

I guess, in that case, you could say I was born into a mix of culture and faith—neither being more or less important than the other. After all, my people say *Caada lagooyo cara Alleey leedahay* or "Broken tradition brings God's wrath."

In terms of religious beliefs, I grew up in a very uniform system. I grew up in a family, in a neighborhood, in a city that was pre-dominantly Sunni Muslim. I left Mogadishu in my early teens, but I had met very few non-Sunnis by that time. We had Sufism, but we had largely what I would call Sunni Sufism. That is, we had Sunni beliefs infused with Sufi practices. We had non-Somalis, but we had mostly Sunni non-Somalis. We had religious classes at school, but they mostly taught the Sunni version of events.

Within Sunnism, we followed the Shafi'i branch or *madhab*. As such, we had cultural connections to other Shafi'is that I didn't even realize were the case until much, much later. For example, men in my culture wore *macawis*, a sarong, and many years later I would visit Indonesia and see that we actually got that from there. Indonesia is predominantly Shafi'i and I understood how their *sarong goyor* became our macawis.

It wasn't the only thing we had in common. Both our women suffered female circumcision because, of course, it is something considered obligatory under Shafi'ism, although most other Muslims do not. But Shafi'is are not a small minority, they compromise about thirty percent of the Muslims around the world.

In other words, I understood that there was a global culture going on, with the faith playing out as a nice bridge. We, as Muslims of Africa, introduced an African practice like female circumcision to our Asian brothers and sisters by getting the practice sanctioned in the Hadiths. They, as Muslims of Asia, introduced us to the Asian way of life, too, through our collaborations.

As a queer Muslim I was also interested in the way culture looked at sexuality. It was interesting to see the relaxed atmosphere for queers in both Somali and Indonesian cultures could also perhaps had its roots in our brand of faith. Shafi'ism does not call for the execution of same-sex participants if the partners are unmarried. Instead, flogging and temporary banishment is preferred—in the rare case that all requirements for such a punishment are met.

In the case of married individuals who do engage in same-sex relationship, execution is the solution.

However, Sha'ifism requires self-confession or the testimony of four male witnesses, who swear on the Qur'an that they have indeed witnessed the act.

In other words, very difficult to prosecute.

But, of course, being a Muslim is much more than faith. Let's talk about Malaysia. Malaysia is also another predominantly Shafi'i country, and yet the atmosphere there is very different from Indonesia.

How comes?

Malaysia was a subject of the British Empire.

Now, let's go back to Somali culture for a little bit. In 1888, the people in northern Somali regions ended up with the British colonial laws as subjects of the British Empire. British Somaliland was the first time we ever had a law against homosexuality in any Somali region.

In 1960, Somali people united and the northern and southern parts, as well as the coastal parts, became a unified and independent country called Somalia. Because southern Somalia was where the majority of the deals were made, says Hadiyo Jim'ale of the Somali LGBT organization Queer Somalis, and because southern Somalia was a former Italian colony, the country became a more Italo-friendly country and therefore the new country did not have laws against homosexuality, as homosexuality had been legal in Italy since 1890.

On the other hand, Hamdi Sultan, a trans activist from Hargeisa, which is the capital of the area the British colonized, says the general constitution might not have had laws against homosexuality but it did not stop the local laws from importing its former sodomy laws into the local ordinance. As a teenager when she moved to Mogadishu, which is the capital of the area the Italians colonized, Sultan recalls being shocked at the different atmosphere there. She saw neighborhoods in which LGBT persons thrived.

However, in 1973 the entire country adopted an Arab League friendly constitution, which included a law against homosexuality, as part of our preparation for the official induction into the Arab World. But even then, it was imprisonment of up to 3 years, and not execution.

"In the 1970s and 1980s LGBT people in the south, therefore, had different experience than the people in the north," says Sultan. "In the south, corrupt police officers would come and black mail those of us who were clearly LGBT, like trans women like myself, but we knew we were not going to be killed by the law. So, they got what they wanted, often our bodies, but we were generally safe."

From 1991 to 2006 there wasn't a central government in Somalia. As such, LGBT people didn't face any legal measures. However, in 2006 the Islamic Courts Union came to power. This immediately began a different course because the Islamic Courts Union was based on a *salafi* system, imported from Saudi Arabia, which meant it didn't adhere to usual branches or madhab.

"Suddenly, you could be executed for being gay or lesbian," says Jim'ale. "The strict interpretation of the Arabian Gulf, which did not interact with our culture for so long, brought a new culture. Whereas we never heard much about homosexuality during Friday prayers before, things changed fast and suddenly the 'evil' homosexuality was a subject of many sermons on Fridays across the country."

In the new Somali central government, the internationally recognized government of the Federal Republic of Somalia that has been operating since 2012, we are back to confusion. At the moment, there aren't any clear laws against homosexuality.

In other words, a gay Somali from the south, who happens to be Muslim, would encounter distinctly different legal experiences under the Italian, Arab World-friendly penal code, Salafi system imported from Saudi Arabia and the new central government.

Did you see how the life of that Muslim changed so drastically?

That is what it means to be a Muslim. Being a Muslim is a personal experience through faith, but otherwise highly influenced by the general society, depending on what kinds of rulings end up affecting your life, first and foremost as the citizen of that country.

My life in the United States as a Muslim is a very different life than my life would have been in Somalia. It would also be different if I was an Iranian immigrant, and I came from a country where the death penalty currently applies to people like myself. But it would also be very different if I were a Turkish immigrant, as Turkey hasn't had any anti-homosexuality laws since the mid 1800s.

Diversity.

History

For my book *Queer Jihad: LGBT Muslims on Coming Out, Activism, and the Faith*, I interviewed Hadiyo Jim'ale, a Somali lesbian and activist who is also featured in this book (see "Today"). During our interview she brought up the story of Al-Amin, the son of Harun al-Rashid, who had taken over the Caliph post in the year 809. She told me about Kauthar, his African lover and whom we both believe to have been a Somali (he was Muslim and came from East Africa, and during that time only the Somali had been Muslim, as they had converted to Islam out of spite against the larger Christian Abyssinia).

If indeed it is true that Kauthar was Somali, it would mean he was the first gay personality that we are aware of in the history of the Somali community.

Of course, there is the mythical Araweelo. According to tradition, she was a Somali queen who believed in the idea of women ruling the world exclusively. She is believed to have had men castrated and would put them in lower level positions in politics. As such, she is deemed a lesbian in the community. I'm not sure if it is because our society can't imagine strong women, or if indeed she was a gay woman.

In the 20th Century, in the age of science investigations, there have been some reports on queer sexualities in the Somali community. According to Will Roscoe and Stephen O. Murray, for example, in their 2001 book *Boy-Wives and Female Husbands: Studies of African Homosexualities* (see page 22), a 1909 book by Austrian anthropologist Friedrich Julius Bieber reported on how Somali men and women, of all ages, commonly practiced mutual masturbation. Bieber also noted that the adult men practiced homosexuality—what he called "uranism," which was a 19th Century term for homosexuality.

In the 1969 book *African Penal Systems*, edited by Alan Milner, there is a chapter entitled "The East African Experience of Imprisonment." In it (see page 302), the author, scholar Ralph E. Tanner, reported on a case of a Ugandan prison in which Somali men had entered the prison with homosexual traits.

In the mid 1980s, when I was a small boy growing up in Mogadishu, I remember people talking about neighborhoods in the old town in which gays lived openly. Hamdi Suldan (see in this book under "Seattle") confirmed those memories for me when I wrote about her in 2001 for the South African queer magazine *Behind the Mask*

It was again confirmed for me in 2002 when I wrote about the story of Ali Abdulle and Ismail Sakariye (see in this book under "Refugees") when I wrote about their ordeal for the multi-lingual African news agency *afrol News*.

Finally, it was also confirmed for me in the mid 2000s when I met Diriye (see in this book under "Washington"), who later shared with me his story. His story, which starts from the 1960s in what is now Kenya, recalls a Mogadishu in which powerful men were openly known to be gay, a time in which the establishment catered to the lesbian community without any troubles from society, and a transgender community where trans women were living open lives.

Of course, I knew none of these things when I was a young teenager in the civil war, living in refugee camps in

Kenya, or being newly immigrant in the United States.

Of course, no one talked about these histories at our dinner tables in Mogadishu, or Nairobi, or Minneapolis. They were just not the kinds of information you learned in school, or from reading good books you easily found in the local bookstores.

Like all histories, queer history matters. This book is about giving people a chance to know about what has been denied to us. Who knew that there were gay religious leaders in our faiths like Caliph Al-Amin, or lesbian queens in our national histories like Queen Araweelo, or openly gay people in our cities like those described by Hamdi Suldan, Ali Abdulle, or Hadiyo Jim'ale?

Now we have these histories, and now no one can deny them. No one can deny us any longer.

Today

Many years ago I met a Somali woman through an online chat room. This was in the late 1990s when Facebook and Twitter had not yet been invented, and people communicated in chat rooms and lists, aside from the anonymous chat lines you called up on the phone.

There was something about the woman, and especially the way she introduced herself to me as "Boston." That was her nickname, she told me. She was a medical doctor in her late thirties living in Boston, Massachusetts, married and with children.

After chatting with her for some time, it came out that she was a lesbian. She never told this information to another man before. After exchanging long discussions about the differences in the communities, as I complained about the promiscuous nature of the mainstream queer male community and she complained about the lack of finding queer women who were just going with the flow of things, we got to the good stuff. "Boston" asked me if I was aware of any support group, either online or offline, that catered to queer Somalis. I felt a deep shame as I told her I didn't know of any such place. I thought maybe I wasn't so into the community and just was unaware.

The truth, unfortunately, was that there were none.

Weeks later, after having discussed important issues that were never really dealt with, I suggested to her that maybe we should start a support group.

"Let's do it," she said, with a little hesitation in her voice.

It took another year or so before we actually took action. In the meantime, I was in the midst of the planning stage for *Huriyah*, a queer magazine that would focus on the issues surrounding Islam and sexuality. I was working alongside several men in Arab countries. Immediately, "Boston" joined us, now as Hadiyo Jim'ale.

It was in late 2001 that we finally got around to starting what would become the first support group ever for queer Somali people. Naturally, after a long battle, we named it "Queer Somalis." It was an online support group. Somewhere you could go and talk in Somali with other queer Somalis and feel okay.

Our group was very small in the beginning. It was less than fifty members that we knew ourselves, some of which were not even Somali. Slowly, it grew into around seven hundred members. These were people from all over the world. We thought we reached our goal, but no one ever imagined what would happen next.

Jim'ale moved back to Somalia, got the organization a vibrant community, and began real work in our community. She ended up meeting the then-president Abdullahi Yusuf, and began going around neighboring countries spreading the message of self love, understanding sexuality, and overcoming societal pressures to confirm to a heteronormative lifestyle.

"Because I realized that most of the people in Somalia were not going to an online group, to discuss the important things that we needed to discuss," says Jim'ale, who has since began going back and forth between Somalia, United Kingdom, and the United States. "Many of them don't have computers and would not feel comfortable doing it in public. Now we have local chapters in Mogadishu, Hargeisa, Bosaaso, and Kismaayo. It is not much but it is small group of people who come together and we help each other."

Today the organization has about a thousand members in six cities. It has participated in conferences in Africa and beyond, has negotiated with politicians for fairer laws, and has saved the lives of countless LGBT people who without it would not have had the critical information they needed to live healthier lives.

The creation of "Queer Somalis," which was both online and offline simultaneously, had been very beneficial to many of us. It encouraged many of us to take the leap and do work in our communities.

Some of the people that formed that group are in this very book, for example. Their lives are now a testament to the lives that will come after them, just as their lives give courage to others like them—both at home and at abroad.

Some of the people from that online group have since started websites, blogs, Facebook pages and groups, and many other things on their own, simply because they were inspired.

The Somali diaspora continuously enriches the lives of the people back home, as their own lives were enriched by the culture they have taken with them elsewhere. The LGBT community is part of that experience. Soon, for example, the world will meet an openly gay Somali imam. Nur Warsame has become Australia's first imam to openly come out of the closet, joining other openly gay imams like Daayiee Abdullah of the United States and Muhsin Hendricks of

South Africa, among others.

The silence has been broken.

Mogadishu

Like all young Somali people, Badal's parents expected him to get married and raise a family at a young age. When at twenty-two he still remained a bachelor, his mother traveled hundreds of miles south of Bosaaso, where they lived, to find him a suitable wife in Galkacyo, where her family comes from and where she knew she could at least find one good girl for her son.

"She didn't hide the fact that she was hunting for a wife for me," says Badal, now 28. "Of course, I was uncomfortable with the idea because I'm homosexual, but what could I have done? This was something everyone did. You got married on your own, or your parents, if you were lucky enough, found you a compatible person to begin your individual journey with."

However uncomfortable he was with the idea of getting married, Badal agreed to it when his mother returned with a beautiful young woman, five years younger than him.

Suddenly, he was the hot shot in the neighborhood as all the guys wanted to take cues from him and his circle of friends seemed to have doubled.

"It was a strange experience," Badal remembers. "I was not popular at all. I mean, I had a few friends but because this girl was so beautiful every guy wanted to be my friend. I think a lot of these guys also thought that I was gay and once I got out of the situation, they could step in and take my place. Opportunists, indeed."

Some of these guys were the same ones who used to call him all sorts of names growing up, says Badal. They called him *lagaroone,* or incompetent, most of the time. But he was called many other things, including faggot.

As a young boy he was beaten a lot by some of these very men and was often excluded from activities because of his perceived weakness.

Badal says he "had a really sad childhood," adding, "I was feeling like an outsider in my own neighborhood—always walking around nervous. No one wanted to be around me, or be my friend. I was like a liability; if you were known to hang with me, you were not going to be allowed into many circles. So, everyone avoided me. It was horrible."

At the age of twenty-two, when his mother was fixing him up in a marriage, Badal was a virgin both to men and women. Up to that point, he had only fantasies about men.

"If I were straight, or at least more masculine than I was, I would have had more action with the boys as they all often masturbated together because girls were off-limits," he jokes.

When the wedding day arrived he was as nervous, if not more, as the bride. In Somalia, brides are always nervous because they have to worry about having sex when they had gone through female genital mutilation and know the first penetration will break their skin—a painful experience.

As a gay man, Badal also had his own fears. He remembers being soaking wet all day. No one gave attention because it was the beginning of the summer months when Bosaaso is really hot.

In bed, however, things were different.

"She really liked me, I guess," he says, laughing. "She was all over me as soon as we got to the bedroom. And this girl was really experienced, I'm sorry to point out. She was not a virgin at all. The funny thing was that, outside the bedroom, no one would ever imagine this 17-year-old conservative girl to be so wild and sexual."

If he hadn't decided he was gay by then, by the morning Badal was convinced he had no business being with women. The entire experience only left him more secure in his own sexuality.

"I had no desire for her whatsoever," he says of his first night with a woman. "I could not wait for it to be over. And she was really into it, and I felt bad because I thought she should be with someone who was as excited about her as she was about me. So I relived all my crushes with the boys that night—just to make her happy. It was a very bad night for me."

A few days later, Badal told his family everything: that he was gay; that he could not be married to the young woman any longer; and that he wanted to just be celibate. He thought celibacy would make things easier.

"I decided that if I can't be with women, then I will just not have sex with anyone. The possibility of being with a man in a relationship didn't cross my mind. I figured it couldn't work in my country, in my culture."

His family was not really surprised, but they couldn't believe their son was telling them these things. His mother was not having any of it. She said that he was suffering from the work of the *shaitan,* the Devil, and proposed that her son get some religious help.

She took him to a sheikh who cured people from all sorts of spiritual and physical illnesses. He had his compound in Qandala (Treanout), an ancient town about 65 miles east of Bosaaso. The sheikh had a huge reputation for curing people of sexual impurities in particular.

"He was very creepy," Badal remembers. "He took one look at me and he wiggled his head. He said I could be cured of my homosexuality, and I wanted to believe so much that he could. I promised to follow his lead, as I really wanted to change."

After several months of therapy that involved everything from the Qur'an being recited over him, sometimes for a whole day non-stop, to being beaten and being forced to smell the smoke from the burning of all sorts of animal feces, Badal realized he was not going to change.

"I still had the same wet dreams, and same fantasies," he says. "Nothing was changing, not even a little. I was growing tired of all these stupid, unbearable so-called treatments. I was sick of it all. I was there for no reason. Inside me, I gave up. I just knew it was not working for me."

One night, while everyone at the camp slept, he sneaked out. He called a friend of his in Mogadishu and asked if he could stay with him for a while. When the friend agreed, Badal was on his way to Mogadishu the next day. He did not contact his family to tell them about his plans.

"I figured the family would not understand," says Badal. "There was nothing for me in Bosaaso but bad memories and shame. Before, it was just rumors and suspicions. Now surely everyone would know I'm homosexual, and I would face disgrace in my neighborhood. Why would anyone ever go back to something like that?"

Badal had never been to Mogadishu. Not before the civil war or after. And he had no idea what to expect. Bosaaso was only affected by the war in a positive way, as its population tripled because of the migration of those who consider it their ancestral homeland, and its economy boomed like crazy. Today, Bosaaso is ten times a better city than before the civil war. Mogadishu, on the other hand, as Badal learned quickly, was another story.

"It was like a horrible scene from a bad movie," Badal remembers. "I got off the bus and I felt completely disoriented by the aura of war. I had never seen anything like that before. There were ruins and bullet holes and everyone looked like they were criminals. I was shocked."

A few days later, he called some friends in Europe and asked for a loan so he could go into business with Duran, his Mogadishu friend. When the people confirmed they would send money, he called his family to tell them that he is safe and living in Mogadishu.

When the money came, he invested with Duran. Years later, they opened two more stores in the *Bakaara,* the second largest market area. Duran was in charge of the first store, Badal was in charge of one of the new stores and they asked a young man to manage the other and in exchange they would share the profits with him.

"His name was Mubarak," recalls Badal. "He was a Reer Xamar (Somali Arab) and very smart. Duran knew him from previous experience, and he felt Mubarak would help us grow faster. I was impressed by the way he spoke of business; it was as if he had a degree or something. It was great."

Not much after they opened the new stores, Badal found himself in a different kind of a relationship with his new business partner.

"I was at the store he managed one night," remembers Badal. "And one thing led to another, and he kissed me. I have never been kissed before. Not like that! I felt like I was melting inside. We went to a hotel that night, and we pretty much made love all night long."

Weeks of love making later, Badal realized he was falling in love with Mubarak. This was particularly dangerous because, aside from the fact that they were in business together, Mubarak was already married and had children. And Mubarak was honest from the beginning that he was not intending to have a relationship with a man and that this was nothing more than sex.

In other words, this was something that was not going to get any more serious than physical. Badal did his best to hide his feelings, and tried to just enjoy the experience. Much to Badal's surprise, however, Mubarak sat him down one night and told him that he was in love himself.

"I could not believe my ears," remembers Badal. "I was crying, he was crying. I told him I was already in love with him, and, man, everything was beautiful—except we didn't know what to do. You know, we asked ourselves what did this mean? Where could we go from there?"

They had no answers. Mubarak reiterated that he would not leave his wife and children. And there was Duran, who was straight, as far as they knew, and what about the business?

"I had a lot invested in the business, and I didn't want to lose it," Badal says, "But I wanted to be with Mubarak."

Also, there was the society to consider. Mogadishu was growing very conservative. Islamism was spreading, and everything was being monitored. There were Islamic courts, which afflicted people with all sorts of Sharia laws and regulations including laws for relationships. They were arresting, torturing and even executing people they felt were criminals, which in their understanding included people who had sex outside of marriage. People were being chastised for silly things like watching sports on television.

"We read stories in the newspapers of homosexuals being executed in Iran and Saudi Arabia," says Badal. "We knew it was possible in Mogadishu, and that was very scary. We decided to be low key, and avoid suspicion. Good thing is that not many people would suspect anything because we are business partners and it is natural we would be together a lot."

Badal knows that in a city like Mogadishu, a city haunted by strife, everyone is really busy with his or her own life. Badal's fears have to do with the things he sees and knows rather than what others may see. In Mogadishu, it is not uncommon for men to be together. In fact, it is suspicious when they are not.

"And we are trying to keep an open mind about it," Badal adds.

Slowly, Mogadishu began to change. Al-Shabaab is no longer in charge. A more humane rule of law is in operation. The city is getting more and more investors moving in, both Somali and non-Somali, and its life is slowly changing for the better.

The neighborhoods are cleaner, and its villas are being renovated. More and more people are feeling prosperous, and it is no longer uncommon to see happy people on the streets. The beaches are open again, and the seafood restaurants are booming.

The LGBT community has also felt that change. Badal is meeting more and more people, and his circle of gay friends is growing. They are connected to the world outside, even though they remain cautious of the future.

Today Badal and Mubarak are still lovers four years after they began their affair. Mubarak stays a few nights with Badal, and fulfills his family obligations most of the week by spending the nights at his house, which leaves Badal feeling restless.

"He does tell me he wants to be with me," says Badal. "But it is hard. Every night he goes to his wife, I hurt even if I don't share that with him."

Baidoa

On the day he was born Abdi wouldn't stop crying until the family's Sufi teacher was called and the first chapter of the Qur'an, the *Al-Fatiha*, was recited over him.

He grew up in the predominately Sufi town of Baidoa or *Baydhabo*, to a well-established family who had ties to the Sufi Tradition both in Somalia and abroad, especially in Upper Egypt, to which they traced their family history. His grandfather had made annual trips to Egypt and returned with Sufi stories.

Abdi had natural talent for the arts and used every opportunity to delve into any kind. He was a singer, for example, singing Sufi songs in the mosque. Then he was painting. But it was really dance that settled in him.

"He danced every single day," remembers Batulo, a childhood friend. "He would dance as a student, and he would dance as a teacher. He would teach us how to dance," she adds, saying that she and other friends learned how to dance from him.

Abdi had the ability to go to a wedding or watch a Bollywood film and be able to instantly recall the choreography. "Then he would infuse it with his own style and make it even better than it was before," says Batulo.

When he was sixteen a local musician invested in him by opening a small dance school where he and Abdi would teach dance and singing, respectively.

In a country like Somalia, where art is often learned at home and not at schools, and where people don't value to invest in art in general, the two first struggled for years.

"It was difficult to make money at first," remembers Hirsi, who saw Abdi at a dance competition and thought he was worth to go into business with. "Abdi believed something would come, and that something was the civil war, which wasn't good for anyone else except us."

The civil war doubled Baidoa's residents, bringing the cosmopolitans of Mogadishu to the art school. Suddenly, the city was flooded with a lot more people who appreciated the arts. Some of the students even had previous classes and were halfway into their chosen fields.

"Despite the daily terror of the civil war, and it was really horrific, our school began to have more and more students," says Hirsi. "We were providing something to make the process easier. These refugees had left everything, and life was becoming more difficult to deal with on a basic level. Yet, here they had something good to look forward to."

However, soon enough the civil war reached Baidoa too. The president was camped in Gedo, and Baidoa was stuck between factions loyal to the president and the rebels from Mogadishu.

The civil war also brought something else: Al-Itihaad, a group of radical Muslims whose teachings resembled more the Wahabbis in Saudi Arabia than the Sufis in Baidoa.

"At first, they opened schools that competed with the Sufi ones," remembers Batulo. "They were very patient, and they really did everything by the book in order not to get the locals all rattled up," she adds. "They were patient for a very long time."

It wasn't until early 2000s that Al-Itihaad transformed itself into the Islamic Courts, which began to make judgments in ways that were a bit foreign to the locals, and later in the mid 2000s it became Al-Shabaab and took over.

"Then everything turned dark," says Hirsi. "They forced us to close the school, and soon our own lives were being threatened if we didn't stop our artistic endeavors. I decided to leave for Kenya, but Abdi refused to give up."

Abdi stayed for another year, but he was becoming more and more depressed. He would stay in the house for days, and everyone began to worry about his well-being.

To make matters worse, his father had been radicalized by that time. As time went on the father became more and more homophobic and began to pressure Abdi to marry.

"It was a joke, because anyone who knew Abdi knew he would never marry a woman," says Batulo, who says she even offered herself to marry him once in order to escape her own soon to be arranged marriage, "Abdi was a wonderful human being, who would never do that to a woman. The sad thing is that the father knew that, but somehow he went along with the advice of his friends."

One day the father said he had found a young woman who was willing to marry the openly gay Abdi, although Abdi's friends suspect that she was being paid by the father to do so.

The night before his wedding, Abdi took his life by ingesting rat poison. He had broken into the building of his former art school, which was in the process of being turned into an apartment building, and was found in the morning by construction workers.

"Abdi's suicide was due to many conflicting things," says Batulo. "Abdi was very openly gay in an environment that was becoming more and more homophobic, but it is not what killed him. What killed him is what kills many of us in this country," she adds. "It is this disease; this foreign disease that is consuming our lives, bit by bit. Our hearts are forced into evil ideas. Our minds are totally being brainwashed. What was once totally abnormal is now totally the normal."

He could have gone elsewhere, exiled himself to Kenya or Ethiopia like many LGBT people from Somalia. Abdi wanted to make a statement. That is why he decided to take his life in his former art school. He used his death as a protest, say friends.

"It is said that there were markings on the ground, indicating he probably was dancing there that night," says Hirsi, his voice breaking. "He wasn't allowed to dance for a while before he died. He must be dancing in heaven now."

Since their son's death Abdi's family had decided to leave the city. They now live in the capital, which is not under the control of Al-Shabaab.

"What happened to Abdi reminds us that LGBT lives are caught in the crossfire of larger issues in society," says Hadiyo Jim'ale, the Executive Director of *Queer Somalis*, the only LGBT Rights organization in the country. "It is not always just homophobia, but it is often also an ailment in the larger society that creates and fosters an environment of hate. What hurts one hurts all. We all have to stand up together."

Baidoa has since become under the leadership of the Federal Government of Somalia, which was established in 2012 at the end of the interim mandate of the Transitional Federal Government (TFG).

"They have had bombings here and there, to remind us the awfulness of their rule," says Batulo, "But I would say Al-Shabaab has lost Baidoa."

Hirsi, who has since moved to Ethiopia, says he plans to return to his city and perhaps start another art school.

"If I do I will name it after my friend," says Hirsi.

Bardera

It is a Thursday evening, about an hour after the sun had set, and a group of Sufis is heading quietly into an unmarked mosque in a field outside of town. It looks more like a farm hut than a *takia*, but this is definitely one important place of worship for these Sufis.

Bardera or *Baardheere*, which is the second largest city in the Jubba Valley, is a place full of contradictions. On the surface it is an agricultural town, and its produce reach as far as Arabia. Like all of Somalia, it professes to be a moderate Sunni city.

Dig a little deeper, however, and you will realize it is actually a Sufi city and its students flock from all nearby towns. There are more Sufi activities going on here than many other parts of the country.

Bardera is in a part of Somalia that was slowly overtaken by Islamic fundamentalism since the early 1990s. Like a lot of towns in southern Somalia, a group called Al-Itihaad arrived in town in 1991, just after a civil war sent the nation into chaos. When Al-Itihaad folded into several groups that ultimately led to the creation of Al-Shabaab in the mid 2000s, it was, of course, natural that its spiritual contradictions only grew.

Bardera is also a town that relies on the kindness of merchants, who bring goods from nearby bigger cities like Kismaayo and Baidoa, for its basic needs such as medicine. Everything, it seems, is imported here.

If one is not privy to these facts, it just all feel a bit off.

That aforementioned group of Sufis, in the meantime, arrives at their unmarked mosque. Female elders had been there since late afternoon, and they have made dinner. They prepared lamb, aromatic rice, and had juiced mangoes.

The Sufi group, whose members come from a diverse tribal background, sit around a delicious meal as one big family. There are elders, adults, young people, and children. Everything moves in complete harmony, and laughter seems to be a constant companion in this little spiritual space.

It is nice to see happy people in a part of the world plagued by sad news, and these people are really happy.

After dinner, everyone is treated to coffee and sweets. It all seems rather like any other Sufi group. That is until a young person is led into the circle, being seated in the middle, and everyone gets quiet and serious. The young person is draped in a beautiful black cloak and has gorgeous feminine face. Yet, the hair is very short, which makes you wonder if it is a boy, as Somali girls generally keep long hair.

"It is neither a boy nor a girl," explains Abshir, a handsome young man who happens to be one of the coordinators of the group. "It is a *labeeb*, who was born into the body of a male but who possesses all the qualities of a female. The age is also very interesting, for surely at fourteen it is neither a child nor an adult."

Soon the teacher commences the evening by reading the Al-Fatiha, the first chapter of the Qur'an, out loud. The students close their eyes and listen to their teacher, who begins creating a spiritual chain, connecting teacher to teacher all the way back to Prophet Muhammad.

"And all the Prophets, all the way to Adam, and to the Angeles, and to the Beloved," he wraps up his chain, to which the students nod and smile. "May the Baraka, the blessing of the evening of evenings, stay present with us throughout."

That is when the labeeb stands up, and recites the Ikhlas, the 110th chapter of the Qur'an, with the most beautiful voice you could imagine. Despite its short verses, the lingering on the important key words in the chapter leave you feeling spiritually fulfilled.

The labeeb follows the Ikhlas with a portion from the 19th chapter, which is entitled "Mary." The story of a young Jewish woman whom God had favored above all else, and who brings forth perhaps the most important personality of her time, leaves everyone teary-eyed.

Abshir tells me the importance of choosing these chapters of the Qur'an. *Al-Ikhlas* in Arabic means "the purifying," and it is a chapter clearly meant to distance Islam from Christianity. *[God] neither begets nor is born*, declares the third verse. At the same time, by accepting Jesus as the Messiah, even if he is seen as a human being, is a way to distance Islam from Judaism.

"We Sufis, in turn, are distant from the rest of the Muslims," explains Abshir. "We are esoteric. We are not interested in politics or forcing people to follow religion. Instead, we are interested in the spirit of the person. We want to learn and teach the tools one needs to satisfy his or her spiritual growth."

Then, just like that, after reciting the Qur'an, the labeeb undresses.

"Oh, my," I whisper to myself, my conditioned mind immediately wondering what is going on. Yet, no one else seems to be surprised or shocked.

The labeeb's nudity releases into the room a sweet smell of a flowery fragrance—something that seems to have been trapped in the lower part of the body, enclosed in the cloak. Then the labeeb closes the eyes and places the balms against the sides of the thighs, in a nervous kind of way.

The labeeb's pose is not any different from a shy or uncomfortable nude model in a class of student painters. Yet, that is not the way these Sufis are watching the labeeb. These Sufi students, led by their teacher, are not observing a subject but a piece of art. They watch as if looking at a captivating painting in a museum. There is so much admiration, almost like they are in awe, and it immediately becomes clear that it is definitely not sexual at all. Everyone looks wherever they wish to look, and whenever they wish to look, and most of them end up looking at the body in its entirety.

As the Sufis observe the labeeb, there are different phrases that are freely thrown around by different members of the group. Some people say things like "What God has willed!" and "God be praised!" and even "The best of creators!"—all of which seem to signal their immense satisfaction with the labeeb's beauty, or being in awe of how God structured the being.

As a Muslim who grew up in this very country, and having been familiar with these phrases all my life, I can't help but feel good about them being applied to a person outside my society's "male" or "female" gender normative.

As a queer activist, whose own involvement to this country had been accompanied by caution at every level, because our very culture is known to be very homophobic, I wonder how these Sufis are in everyday life towards other queers whose sexual or gender identities might not fit with the society.

After thirty minutes of so, the teacher begins to recite the Al-Fatiha again, and is joined by the students who yet again close their eyes and listen to the beautiful verses. Afterwards, the labeeb clothes back again and sits down in the circle. One by one, the entire group goes to the labeeb where they shake and kiss the hand, and greet with the familiar greeting of "Peace be upon you."

"Now we take a short break," says the teacher, who smiles and nods at the labeeb, who takes the cue and gets up, and is escorted away by an elderly lady that I later found out was the grandmother.

Everyone mingles and they begin to talk amongst themselves in small groups. The conversations seem to center on the experience—the labeeb, the beauty of creation, and how they feel one with the Divine.

"We have just witnessed the beauty," explains Abshir, who tells me how the practice of *shahid bazi*, or what has been translated to mean witnessing the great beauty in Farsia, dates back to the Sufis of Persia. "We have heard, we smelled, we saw, we touched, and we tasted. We have mesmerized all of our senses with that which had been created by the best of the creators," he adds, smiling. "We have satisfied the soul's need to be reminded of such beauty."

The Arabic phrase *ahsan ul khalaqeen*, which means

"the best of creators," is a phrase that appears in the Qur'an in Chapter 23 verse 14. The Sufis, according to Abshir, believe that human beings are co-creators with God in smaller ways, in terms of scientific advancement or even shaping the planet for the better, but that the Divine remains the best of creators.

"Of course, our limited power in co-creating can also harm us," explains Abshir. "We think we are so powerful and we end up falling victim to our own ego," he adds. "This is a reason to turn to spiritual maintenance. Sufism is a tool to help the soul remember its place. Witnessing beauty is just a small part of our larger experience as Sufis. We also commune together, we do individual spiritual exercises, and we spend some time also doing absolutely nothing."

The labeeb was born in Beled Xaawo, a town in the same state and on the Kenyan and Ethiopian borders. The labeeb was born as Abdirahman, a name bestowed upon the little baby by the grandmother. The woman's only daughter had complications and died in childbirth, but she was so grateful that she decided to give the baby a namesake that would remind her about the mercy that she was afforded. So, she named the baby a popular name that has the meaning of the Servant of the Merciful in Arabic.

"Mommy," as the labeeb called her, since she was the only mother the labeeb had ever known, "I think I'm a girl," heard the grandmother one evening, which led her to question the little five year old and got the confirmation of something she had already known for some time—that her grandson was not a boy at all.

"She visited several witchdoctors," Abshir says. "She

wanted to find a way to cure the little boy and keep him as a boy, and let him grow up with a 'normal' life. They tried many things, but nothing worked for her. She began to accept the child and began to seek alternatives."

Then, as luck would have it, she had heard of a group of Sufis who delight in such beings. She would have to move to Bardera, and the baby would grow up and serve the community. She could live in a community that respected her child, and she could watch the importance of its life.

"But, of course, we don't want children," says Abshir, making sure people understand that this is a very unique situation. "She knew she would have to raise the child on her own, and that he or she would only become important to us for maybe a year or two. We explained to her that when he or she would become of adult age, we would no longer be in need of that service."

In other words, the grandmother moved to Bardera, raised Abdirahman until this "in-between" age, and would soon see her grandchild being replaced by another. So what happens to Abdirahman after the age of adulthood? Abdirahman will have the choice to become a member of the Sufi group, doing some sort of permanent service like cooking or cleaning, or Abdirahman will be given some money and will go somewhere else.

"Many of these kinds of people go to big cities like Mogadishu or Hargeisa," says Hadiyo Jim'ale, the Executive Director of *Queer Somalis*, a support group for LGBT Somalis that is based in Somalia. "Some leave the country and go to Kenya or Ethiopia, or perhaps to Arab countries. No matter where they go, however, they often end up becom-

69

ing prostitutes. Many of them will die on the streets, killed by homophobic lovers. It is a sad situation."

A year later, Abdirahman, who was never allowed to join the Sufi group before, opted for joining the group when his days as a witnessed beauty expired. Knowing that a life of ridicule would wait as a female, Abdirahman chose to "become" a man and asked me to represent him as such. For Abdirahman, it meant he would have some respect in his situation.

"I'm okay with that," he says.

Soon enough, Abdirahman is coaching the next labeeb in line, which interestingly enough happens to be a boy who was born in the body of a boy. A similar boy preceded Abdirahman also, and Abshir explains that is because it is very rare to find a "real" labeeb.

"The labeeb, you could say, is the top of the line," says Abshir, who insists this not a discrimination against boys who are born into boys' bodies. "It is just that they offer such ambiguity that it makes the process that much more interesting."

Interesting, indeed.

Brava

It was only just a little after nine in the morning and Nuuroow's day was already almost over. He had gone into the waters around sunrise, which happened to be three-and-half hours earlier. He was very successful; he caught around a dozen large fishes, and will sell everything by eleven when the ladies finish their daily shopping.

After lunch, like many young people in this coastal town, Nuuroow takes a long nap that lasts several hours.

By late afternoon, he usually hangs out near the beach, relaxing in the shade and enjoying the breeze. If things go his way, which he admitted is often the case, he would meet another young man and they will have sex after dinner.

"Yes, this is my life," Nuuroow, who is just twenty-three, laughed in his blue room in the center of town.

But gay life was extremely dangerous at the time in Brava or *Baraawe*, where Islamist groups including Al-Shabaab had been in power since the 1990s. Over the years, they have lashed many men and have even executed some, as the married ones are often killed while the single men are lashed hundreds or even thousands of times.

"Baraawe is now their strongest town," Nuuroow told me at a time when the radical Islamist group Al-Shabaab was in full power. "Of course, we are still living our lives, and we defy them at every chance we get," he added, as he smiled at a waiter in a nearby cafe with whom he had hooked up before. "This is my town."

Nuuroow was born in Baraawe, and grew up in a town

broken by various occupiers since the national government was dismantled in 1991. Some of the occupiers have been more merciful than others, but none has been as fear inducing as the Al-Shabaab, whipping the town into submission.

Soon, Nuuroow was chatting up the guy from the cafe and the two agreed to go to a party together later that evening. The waiter was finishing work an hour later, and they had the time to have sex before the party.

On the way to the party Nuuroow ran into his father. He and his father had been having issues, as Nuuroow had turned down the arranged marriage to one of his cousins and the father took the situation personally. The father, who has been the leader of the family's charcoal export business, had long hoped his son would take over the family businesses.

"I don't want to send our burn trees to Pakistan," Nuuroow had told his father years earlier.

Despite their issues the father stopped and talked to his son for a few minutes. Of course, by the way Nuuroow was dressed and how good he had smelled the father could gather his son was on his way to a party.

"Parties are the only way we survive here," Nuuroow said to me. "They give us the much-needed breeze from the torching sun called Al-Shabaab. Without these parties we would have no life. They have to be underground, and very discreet, but it is normal life for us now."

The party, which took place in a private residence in the Baghdad neighborhood of the town, was busy with young men. It was a place to meet, and some of these kids were coming from other towns even. In the background, there were Bollywood songs re-imagined in Bravanese language. It was rather interesting listening to Abdulahi Burci singing Kumar Sanu numbers. Although the music itself was basically electronic stuff, made in the computer of a local producer, Burci's voice made up for everything.

"We are very close to the Indian culture," explained Nuuroow, who identifies as an Indian-Somali mix because he believes his people are descendants of Indians. "Their music sounds very natural to us, and we have very similar way of life."

Although the language of the Bravanese people, officially called Chimwini by linguists, has been a part of the larger Swahili language, more and more linguists are classifying is as a stand-alone language and not necessarily a dialect of Swahili. They reason that there are borrowed Somali, Arabic, and Swahili words in the language but that it actually is a language of its own with its own unique words and system. Many Bravanese people agree with this assessment.

In terms of the way they look, the majority of the Bravanese people tend to be more light-skinned than the mainstream Somalis. On their faces you might recognize traces of their city's past locals—the Arab Muslim migrants, the Portuguese invaders, the Indian merchants, et cetera.

Of course, stay a little longer at the party and you will hear the musical connections make their way. Cesária Évora remixed by a local DJ into Arabic groove? No problem! Oum Kalthoum tuned into Bollywood beats? Let's dance some more! Asha Abdow in Samba mix? Oh, my!

Parties like that are the lifeline of many of the towns

that were controlled by Al-Shabaab, tells me Nuuroow. They are often held in a house, music is not too loud, and they prefer that people come into the house one at a time. As such, they tell different groups to come at different times, to avoid a crowd outside the house.

I found their bravery to be incredible. These gay men and women were really living lives on the edge. One word to the local Islamists and they would all have been thrown in jail; everything in that house was illegal. The music, the dancing, the sensuality, the smoking of *xashiish* or hash, the Kenyan beer, everything they were doing was illegal.

"Another night of making it to safety," said Nuuroow, as he returned to his apartment late at night with his waiter friend. "I will have couple of hours of sleep before tomorrow starts all over again. But not before I cum again," he laughed.

Kismayu

The *Dalxiis*, which literally means "vacation" in Somali and was a government-controlled recreational park in the north of the city, welcomed you to Kismayu or *Kismaayo*. It was a beautiful coastal area, filled with exotic flowers from all over the country, and maintained with a western-style gardening system.

For Adan, who grew up in Jamaame, which is a town around forty miles from Kismaayo, it was the perfect welcome to the city. He was nineteen, and it was the first time he went to the big city.

"I was happy to be coming," says Adan, now in his early forties. "It was something I had been dreaming of since I heard all of those stories as a young boy."

But the park was not the only thing that welcomed him. As he wandered around the place, obsessed by all the interesting architecture, he saw another young man and the two began to eye each other in a friendly way. They struck up a conversation, and soon they were having sex in the other young man's room, in his family's rented vacation flat in the park.

Although the sex was very good, it was what happened after sex that made the time special. Adan says it was as though he met his long lost brother or friend, and he knew whatever it was needed to be repeated again and again.

"Unfortunately, his family returned to Mogadishu the very next day," remembers Adan, sadly, "I never saw him again. But I also never, ever forgot the experience. I guess you never forget your first time."

Now that he had lost his virginity in the city, drawing on an old superstition, Adan says he became attached to Kismaayo. Originally, he was only going to stay for a few days and return home.

"I changed my mind," he remembers, laughing, "I began to chase that feeling, and I was hanging out in Calanleey, and it was not hard to find horny guys at all," he adds. "I sometimes had two or three guys in one day. Those were the days before we lost it all in the chaos of the civil war."

Calanleey, which is a popular beach neighborhood, is a melting pot of cultures, bringing Somali, Swahili, and Arabic cultures together. It is also the oldest part of the city and has a long tradition of been the city's gateway to the world outside.

Adan fell in love with the neighborhood, its multicultural lifestyle, and the plentiful of sexual experiences he found there. He immediately got himself a job, working as a waiter at a neighborhood restaurant, and moved in with a few other gay men into a small house.

"The house was very old," remembers Adan, showing me pictures of a beautiful little house on a hill of many other little houses, "I have such fond memories of the place," he adds, "I had great sex there, almost everyday."

It was then he met another young man named Mursal. Mursal was from that neighborhood and he never even had sex with other men, and wasn't sure if he could. Slowly, and without Adan pushing for it, their friendship turned into something else. The two couldn't help but feel the way they did, and sex only confirmed what they suspected—that they were already in love.

"Mursal had his own place, and I moved in with him," remembers Adan. "We lived in that place together for couple of years before the civil war tore everything apart."

Mursal belonged to a tribe that was chased out of Kismaayo in 1991, and he never returned. He ended up in Kenya, and then in South Africa, where he contracted HIV and eventually died from AIDS.

"I think about him often," says Adan, smiling at a photo of Mursal, who seems happy in the photo, "I know what would have happened had he stayed, we would have been together today."

But Adan is also very much in love with the current man in his life, a wealthy man in his late fifties named Guhaad, who is married and who has no hope of ever living the kind of life Adan would like.

"I love him still," says Adan, who says the two are together most of the time, "I don't like it in my head that I'm with a married man, but I love him. He makes me smile, and I know he goes out of his way to give me happiness."

Officially, Adan lives alone. But if you look at his closet, you will find half of the clothes belong to Guhaad, and Guhaad drives Adan's car more than Adan does. Guhaad's family, his wife and grown children, had met Adan many times, and they all pretty much know what is going on.

However, Guhaad comes and goes whenever he pleases, in both houses. Some nights he leaves Adan late and goes over to his family, and some nights he stays there all night. He almost always eats lunch with the family, but he always has dinner with Adan.

"It is surreal life for someone like you, someone conditioned by the Western way of life," says Adan to me when I question him about how he manages that kind of life with Guhaad, "I don't really think about much of his life, I live my life. He is in it, but I don't think about the life he has without me."

Adan says Guhaad's wife never demands anything, because she had seen the difference in her husband. She knows that he is happier with Adan. She knows if she asks for a divorce that Guhaad would give it to her without any hesitation. So, to keep the life he provides for her, she goes along with sharing him.

"But she knows he will never divorce her on his own," says Adan, rolling his eyes the way a jealous lover would. "They are related, she is his distant cousin, and so it would never be something he would do. As long as he gives me what I need, the love and time I deserve, I'm basically okay with it, I guess."

It seems to work for everyone.

Hargeisa

At a wedding, full of every age and every gender, two women dance together. They *niikis* together, rubbing their torsos on each other. Their joy has become one, their garments can no longer be separated, and you would be hard pressed to point out which of the two sweats into the other more.

Dirty, dirty dancing.

Yet, these are straight women. Such is the story of Somali women in the north and the complete freedom they have to sensually play with each other in public, unlike men. If two men were doing the same thing, they would be attacked without a doubt.

During *buraanbur*, or women's poetry, there are always two women dancing together—sometimes as close as two people can be, sharing one *garbisaar* or shawl, under which God only knows what they are doing.

Although Somalis consciously do not separate men and women the way some other Muslim folks do, naturally Somali women find themselves in the company of other women. This tends to be in several special places.

For example, in the kitchen it is almost always women. In many families, men are not allowed there or even to cook in general.

Laundry spaces are also women-only areas, generally. There are dry cleaners where men might run the front part of the store, but it is always women in the back doing all the hard work.

At weddings, it is women who are doing the beautiful poetry. Women also do everything related to the bride such as beautification and even preparation for sexual life.

At sacrifices and feasts, it is always women who are preparing the large quantities of food for the people. They also often distribute the food to the local neighborhood.

It is also almost always the case that unmarried young women share beds.

Isfahan and Shamsa are lesbian lovers and first cousins. They lived together at their uncle's house in Mogadishu until they were in their late teens. They shared beds. When Shamsa was nine, 12-year-old Isfahan woke her up one night with tender kisses.

"And we have been lovers since that night," tells me Shamsa. Well, that was twenty-two years ago. "It has been such an amazing road of love for both of us."

Their families believe they are "friends" because they always chose to be together. At their uncle's house, tells me Shamsa, there were four other cousins and the two always chose to do housework on the same day, always shopped for the family on the same day and danced together at weddings at the same time.

It may sound funny to a non-Somali that no one suspected anything, but there is nothing to suspect about a relationship like that in the Somali community. Straight women are doing that all the time.

The only way it would be suspicious is if their behavior continued after marriage, and neither of them has agreed to marriage just yet.

"There have been offers from relatives," says Isfahan, who is now aged thirty-four, which is plenty beyond the marriageable age for Somali women. "It has never been the right one. The day they offer me Shamsa, I will agree," she adds, laughing.

The coupled lived together in Italy for over ten years, and developed their own family. They shared a two bedroom flat in southern Rome with their cat. Both of them worked for a wealthy Italian family, which allowed them to spend a lot of time together. Isfahan was the maid and Shamsa personal assistant to the family matriarch.

In a situation like that, in Italy, they would have lived at the home of their employer. However, the two wanted to have their own lives.

"We wanted to have work life separate from the other areas of our lives," says Isfahan, who used the second bedroom as her office—working on novels, textiles, and other interests like photography.

Their work life was also a time of intimacy, although the Italian family, who apparently were very homophobic, was not aware of their relationship.

"It made a big difference," says Isfahan. "We speak in Somali which the family doesn't understand and it helped us live as openly as we could."

They had moved to Hargeisa together. There, they met some other lesbians and now they share a seven-bedroom house with four other couples. Ten lesbians under one roof.

"It is so much fun," says Shamsa, laughing. "We all have sex at the same hour." I gasp and she adds, "I'm joking!"

Hargeisa, which is safer than most cities in the area, is booming with businesses and all the lesbian roommates own shops in a little mall together. "We actually make more money in our own country," says Isfahan, who manages the finances for the couples. "It is a beautiful country and we love living at home."

Coming back to the Somali community as a lesbian is not an easy choice. You are literally risking your life. Not far from Hargeisa, two lesbians were put to death in 2001—all because they wanted to get married. You could be forced to marry a man, which is something that happened to a friend of the couple. Shamsa and Isfahan are aware of these risks. Yet, they had deep love for their country.

"It is definitely worth it," says Isfahan. "As they say, there is no place like home."

Refugees

As a young gay boy Ali read a lot. He mostly read novels, he says. The concept of soul mates always seemed to be a present thought in the genre he was interested in, romance. Ali, however, really didn't believe in it. At the age of ten, his family had to move. The decision was hard for the family, who lived in the neighborhood they were moving from for almost twenty years.

"I remember mother cried," says Ali. "It was very hard leaving all of our friends and neighbors."

The new neighborhood was what it was expected to be. It was new and foreign. The family had to start from scratch. This is where Ismail, then an 11-year-old, comes into the story. Ali's family moved next to Ismail's. The two kids naturally went to the same school. They became friends.

"We became friends rather quickly," remembers Ismail. "I never made friends that fast. We just had more in common than either of us anticipated."

The boys found out they liked and disliked just about the same things. But what really brought them together, remembers Ali, was their common dislike for sports.

A year after meeting the boys had "accidental" sex one night.

"We were just playing and it just happened," says Ismail.

Well, it happened and happened and happened again. For another three years the boys had sex on a regular basis.

In Somalia it is not uncommon for boys to have sex with each other. What is uncommon, however, is that these boys' sexual "experiments" had gone beyond the age they are usually expected to stop. At the age of 16 and 17, the boys were still having sex.

"After a certain time, I couldn't imagine living without him," Ali says.

So, love came and knocked on their doors.

To fall in love with a man when you are expected to marry a woman is a big problem, most of all with you. At the age of eighteen, Ismail's family had proposed that he marry a third-cousin of his. The boy was overwhelmed and told the family he was gay.

All hell broke loose.

Ismail's family, who are religious Sunni Muslims, believed homosexual acts would condemn their son to a lifetime of hell in the world to come, and cruel and painful punishment in this life.

"Oh, they were way so angry. My father was in a full rage and was running around with a knife," says Ismail. "It was far more than I thought it would be. It was crazy. I can't even begin to tell you how they all seemed like they were about to explode."

Though Ismail did not out his lover, the couple were forced to deal with the situation. It wouldn't take much to put two and two together and to figure out the boy he had been spending so much time with is his lover.

"I was extremely in love with him," Ali says. "There was

no way I was going to watch them kill him. We had to do something."

They did something, all right. They ran away together to another city.

"Ali just came to my bedroom late one night and he had a bag with him," remembers Ismail, laughing through it all. "I remember I looked at him and said 'where are you going?' and he said 'we are going to Shalaamboot.'"

The young couple was told that Shalaamboot, a town about seventy miles south of Mogadishu, was an accepting place they could move to. They could live there, and enjoy being around others in the LGBT community, they were told. It was their only hope of ever being together.

Yet, soon enough their dream town became an ugly nightmare when the couple learned they would have to make some changes to their appearances.

"After we arrived in the city, we found this lady that we were looking for. She put us in her home and was very nice," remembers Ali, who was related to the woman. "And then she casually went into town. When she returned, she returned with a bunch of men dressed in women's clothing."

Drag Queens? Not exactly. In some communities in parts of Somalia, especially in the south, which has had a lot of history with non-Somalis, gay men are expected to either remain in the closet or wear women's attire, especially *shuko* or a chador.

"Of course, the choice was clear," Ismail says. "We told them we would just be in the closet then."

A whole new world was possible for the couple. They were in a city where they had the choice to be in the closet.

"We really didn't care to not be out as long as we were together," says Ali. "We couldn't have asked for a better situation. In Somalia. Together. Safe. All things we never thought were possible after Ismail came out."

The couple, however, was shocked when it turned out that the local community was not happy with their decision. The locals, who were not all queer, decided to boycott the couple. It started with their good hostess kicking them out. Then they couldn't even find a place to rent or a job in the gay friendly neighborhood. They had to live with a supportive woman, secretly, and far from the area they would have preferred.

Although they lived far from the gay friendly neighborhood, the young couple went there everyday, walking almost an hour to reach there. They had hoped to find a better situation, and it was becoming less and less friendly.

Weeks of agony and fear followed that. The couple was running out of money, as money got tight when the grocers in the gay friendly neighborhood would not even sell them anything. The young couple was forced to eat at tourist restaurants, which was chipping away at their little savings.

"We only had money we could survive on a week or two," says Ismail. "We were getting scared we would not even have enough to return to Hamar [Mogadishu.]"

Suddenly the "accepting" town has become the young men's worst nightmare. It was time to reconsider things.

"I proposed we just go to another city," remembers Ali,

who was against the idea of even considering having to go drag. "I was up for anything but becoming a Drag Queen. I told Ismail that I would rather die."

Love conquers all, a concept so ever-present in the books Ali read, was suddenly becoming less and less true.

"They were killing our thoughts, our souls," says Ismail. "I thought we should reconsider their offer. It was the only choice."

The town elders have made an offer to the couple. The offer, to live in the town and be supported as long as they made changes to their attire, seemed outrageous to Ali.

"Ismail helped me see that we could beat them in their own game," remembers Ali, who after a while decided to go with Ismail's plan of agreeing to the attire while the couple would not do it in the privacy of their home. "Then we went to them and told we wanted to take up on their offer."

The ban was lifted and the couple was immediately provided with a job and a place to rent.

They got smart. They matched their working hours, and they stayed in the rest of the day together. While they stayed in, they dressed as men.

"You have no idea how much wearing a pair of jeans means to you in that situation," says Ali, laughing. "I would start undressing when my eye could see the first glimpse of the house. You simply can't wait."

What is with all this fuzz about clothing? Many Somalis believe gay men are imitating women, say the couple.

"It is their way of making us pay for being gays," adds

Ismail. "You make up all these beliefs to punish people who you disagree with. It was like 'damn you for being a queer.'"

About ten years after I originally wrote this story I finally learned what this was all about. In Lower Shabele, and especially towns close to Merca, wearing chador was traditionally a way to beat the system: if you were in a chador no one could suspect you're gay—certainly not from your swishing, if you were to swish. As such it was originally something transgendered women and feminine gay men had used.

"The neighborhood was just protecting itself by having gay men wear these things," explains Dahir Ahmed, a man from Merca, "It was not meant to punish them in any way."

Dahir Ahmed further explained to me that the chador had become a symbol of the discreet. The area where these boys were living, the gay "friendly" area, was an area known to the town as the place to go if you were interested in homosexual activities but did not identify as homosexual.

"It is the area of town to find your lady boys," says Dahir Ahmed, "It is a big business, so obviously your friends were too young to understand what was really going on."

When the civil war broke out in 1991, the young couple ditched the drag and immigrated to neighboring Kenya.

"I think we are the only ones who are grateful for the civil war," says Ismail, who admits he is joking. "I was just so happy to leave there. We lived in a bad situation back there."

Once in Kenya, they applied for asylum as refugees. Three years after their application, they arrived in the United States.

"We didn't know you could apply for asylum back then," says Ali, laughing. "If we knew that, we would have come earlier than that, even when Somalia was still okay. But we are here now and that is all that matters."

Now far away from all that, in a land where they are told 'be all you can be,' Ali wholeheartedly believes Ismail is his soul mate. He realizes that life can bring you good out of what seem like unthinkable situations.

"That first move was hard on me, but it brought me love," says Ali. "That civil war put us through the hell of having to be refugees, but it brought us freedom."

The universe does work in mysterious ways. Well, at least for this couple.

Nairobi

When Sahra immigrated to Kenya, from Somalia, after a civil war broke out in her country, she had no idea she would find love there.

"I didn't even know I wanted to love," says Sahra, who accepts herself as a lesbian. "I didn't even know I could love."

At the age of seventeen her family arrived in Nairobi, Kenya's capital. Sahra was clueless about Kenyan culture, as were most Somalis.

"We didn't know how to deal with these people," she says, "or how they would deal with us. We were scared, though we knew it was a lot better than where we came from."

Kenya didn't want foreigners. It couldn't even employ all of its citizens, and the Kenyan government believed foreigners, unless they came to help the Kenyan society, were anything but helpful. So, Kenya always deported illegal residents.

Somalis were refugees and the United Nations sponsored them into camps, generally in the northeastern part of the country, near the border with Somalia, where food and shelter were available to them.

"Many of the Somalis who came to Kenya mainly led lives of luxury prior to the civil war," says Sahra, whose father was a former minister in the government. "Living in camps was not an appealing option. We wanted to stay in Nairobi."

About a month after Sahra's family arrived, Kenya launched an all-out deportation campaign, referred to as *raaf* in the Somali community.

"I was caught on my way to buy milk from a kiosk [a small grocery store]," says Sahra, whose family was not aware of what was taking place. "I wasn't even given the time to tell my family of what happened to me."

She was taken to a nearby police station. She was told she would spend the night there, and the next morning she would be deported.

Terrified, after learning of what was going on, her family searched for their daughter, with the help of some Kenyan-Somalis, referred to as *Sijjui* by the non-Kenyan Somalis. The family could bribe their way into the prison and get their daughter out the next morning before she was deported. But, not before something extraordinary happened to the young woman.

"The place was filled with non-Somalis," says Sahra, laughing. "I was put in the wrong cell, I guess. I was the only Somali there."

Sahra, who could speak English, befriended some of the other women. They talked about where they came from and shared their experiences.

One of the cellmates, a Kenyan woman named Mary, said she was falsely arrested for being a prostitute.

"I'm, as I was then, a lesbian," said Mary, to the women, which Sahra did not understand, as it was a term that was rather new to her. "Why would I bother with being a prostitute? Don't you have to enjoy your work to be something like that? The irony is that in Kenya real prostitutes are not arrested at all."

Sahra says she doesn't know why she instantly believed in Mary that night, despite the fact that the two women did not know each other.

"I guess, I could just feel she was telling the truth," shares Sahra. "She just seemed like the sort of person who would not lie. She was very kind to me."

Mary says she found Sahra's belief in her illuminating.

"I always assumed Muslims did not like non-Muslims," says Mary, who considered herself Catholic, even though she really didn't practice any religion anymore. "In my heart, I apologized to all Muslims for the assumption later that night."

Mary thought Sahra's accepting of everyone was refreshing, which led the two, though against the rules, to stay up talking almost until dawn. It was after everyone went to bed that Mary whispered a secret to Sahra's ear.

"She said something and I didn't hear it," recalls Sahra. "Then she said she was lesbian. I didn't know what that meant. Then she explained and I said 'oh.'"

Sahra says she knew she was exactly what Mary explained a lesbian to be. However, she recalls, she didn't feel confident enough to say the same thing. Rather, she realized why she had believed in Mary so strongly.

"I think I realized at that moment that there was something going on between us," says Sahra, laughing. "It was very obvious. I think we both knew exactly what we wanted to do with each other, but we didn't."

Mary gave Sahra her phone number. And the women are together ever since.

"Meeting Mary was the best thing that ever happened to me," says Sahra, who returned to Kenya for Mary three years after she and her family arrived in the United States. "I knew I had to be with her. Love her. It wasn't a choice I had to make, but a path I had to follow."

Sahra realized she would never be able to bring Mary to America, as it was long before Same-Sex Marriages became legal in the United States. The decision to go back was hard, as Sahra did not have any prospects of making a living in Kenya, but it was something she had to do, she says.

With her father's help, as he gave her a big loan, she opened a clothing store in the heavily Somali-populated Nairobi district of Eastleigh. Now, combined with Mary's secretarial income and money Sahra receives from her family in the United States, the couple lives a nice life.

"It is nothing like life in the States," says Mary, who visited Sahra several times while she was in America on temporary visas. "But we have love. That is more than enough."

Sahra says living with Mary has given her so much happiness she would otherwise have missed in America.

"I'm the happiest woman in Kenya," she says, giggling. "My dreams are coming true. I'm with the one I love. For that, I'm grateful."

Cape Town

When Deko was born, in Kenya in 1986, his parents named him Mohamed, after the Prophet. He was sick often, and all the mainstream doctors had given up on curing him, so his parents took him to a religious man.

"He suggested that they change my name to Ibrahim," says Deko, who now lives in South Africa, in honor of another Islamic Prophet that is believed to have found 'healing' from the disease of ignorance when he embraced the idea of God.

Unfortunately, Deko had an older brother named Ibrahim. To differentiate the two, as two Somali brothers would never like having the same name, the religious man added Deeq to the end of Ibrahim, and so Mohamed became Ibrahim Deeq.

Finally, as a young boy, he acquired another name. This time, a nickname, Nunkish, because he was the tenth and last child in his family.

So, "my name is confusion," jokes Deko.

Another confusion came in the form of national identity. He was born in Garissa, a city in northeastern part of the country, which is generally populated by Somalis.

"Even though I was a national of Kenya, I never felt like Kenyan," remembers Deko. "The flood of refugees from Somalia led to the frequent raiding of our homes, where the police would come looking for illegal immigrants. We were forever being told to produce our identification papers, to prove we were Kenyan. They treated us with brutal disrespect, and would search our house as if looking for drugs."

When he came to South Africa people would ask his birth date. Deko, although he knows he was born in 1986, has no idea the exact date.

Then, finally, it was his sexuality. He grew up bullied, both at home and in school. In school, both teachers and students would taunt him, calling him degrading names like *shoga*, which pretty much would translate to faggot.

"I felt like the whole town knew I was different, and I hated being there. Every corner I passed I would be called names," he says.

As he grew up the confusion lessened. It all started when one day he overheard people talking about South Africa, and how same-sex couples could get married there.

"They were disgusted by it, but I felt this was the place I would like to live in," says Deko, who from that day began investigating how he could ever go there.

By mid teens he was on his way to South Africa. He arrived in Tanzania, where he spent about ten months, and then moved over land through countries like Zambia and Swaziland before finally arriving the country of his dreams.

"In South Africa I had many struggle, and ups and downs, but a big part of me loves being here," he says. "I have met people I never could have in Kenya, and had experiences which have enabled me to grow and learn."

One of these experiences was losing his faith. Deko had a very difficult time to reconcile his sexuality and faith, leading to leave Islam and try other faiths, which didn't seem to have been all that different from Islam.

Later, he reconnected with his faith through a local queer Muslim organization led by an openly gay imam named Muhsin Hendricks.

"Everything started to make sense spiritually for me," says Deko. "Today I regard myself as a spiritual person who practices Islam, without contradiction."

Deko is no longer confused about anything. He accepts himself as a queer man, in a happy marriage with another man, and has recently taken to YouTube to come out to his family and the Somali community worldwide.

Jeddah

It is an early morning, just before dawn, in Ramadan, and Shukri and Dahabo are in a hurry to eat their last meal of the night, their *suhuur*. They're hurrying because they had to first serve the family they work for, and only then could they eat themselves.

They are maids, and they are a couple.

"We are an unusual couple," laughs Dahabo, a 41-year-old Somali-born lesbian who has been a maid most of her life. "Being a maid is definitely not an easy job," she adds, "I'm very happy to have found someone who makes life better."

In the northern suburbs of Jeddah, where the women work, life is all about luxuries and liberties. This part of Jeddah is definitely a different kind of Saudi Arabia than most people imagine. There are parties happening almost every night. Young people are living lives just as crazy as their counterparts in New York City or Paris.

Yet, there is a serene part of culture here such as the beach, the slow life, and the seclusion of compounds. Regardless of how serene it is, however, these women don't want to tempt fate.

"Being a lesbian is much easier than being a gay man in this country," says Dahabo, who has some gay friends, both male and female. "But we are still very cautious. For example, our bosses have no idea we are a couple, they just think we are cousins."

They may sound like kissing cousins, but these two are

not cousins at all. However, in a country like Saudi Arabia, where racism is a normal and historical part of the culture, nobody cares about who they are, their relationship, or even their religion.

"If you do a good job, you're often left alone here," says Dahabo, "I know it is not always the case with every family," she adds, "I've heard of awful stories of families abusing their maids."

Dahabo has been in Saudi Arabia since 1983. She has had many jobs before she started working for this family in 1989. Some of these jobs included being a maid to a Somali family, oddly enough where the mother of the family was a maid herself to a rich family.

"I was very young, and I wasn't ready to be hired by the Saudis just yet," explains Dahabo. "The Somali family was going to be the perfect start to my new life."

Except that with his wife working most of the day, the husband began bothering the young Dahabo. She threatened him that if he didn't leave her alone she was going to report him to his wife.

"Then he backed off," remembers Dahabo.

After that experience Dahabo made an effort to learn Arabic and began to slowly grow in her profession. However, in 1989 she hit it big, she says, when a wealthy family hired her. It immediately changed her life.

At the time, this family was composed of only the young couple that had just gotten married. They had fired their first maid mere days before they hired Dahabo.

"Since then, they had seven children," recounts Dahabo, who says she sees the children far more than their own mother. "Over the years, the staff grew, and at one point they needed to hire another maid."

That is how 31-year-old Shukri, whose mother is Somali and father is Ethiopian, came into the picture. Six years earlier she was hired as the junior maid, to help the overwhelmed Dahabo with the maid duties.

At first, things weren't so smooth between the women. Shukri was defensive, thinking Dahabo was using her seniority to make her do all the hard work. Dahabo, on the other hand, worried Shukri might be a bit lazy.

"Once I figured out she was just trying to help me do a good job," says Shukri, who was offered the job because Dahabo knew her aunt and told the family they were cousins, "I calmed down, and ever since we have had a very nice working relationship."

However, they soon realized their tension was more than job related. Indeed, there were a lot of pressure with starting a new job for Shukri, and Dahabo having had to learn how to work with someone else, but there were other reasons as well.

The women were also secretly attracted to each other!

"I had already known about my sexuality for a long time by then," says Dahabo, who has had relationships with women before. "This was a different story for her. She hadn't dealt with her sexuality at the time, and she was very confused."

After weeks of confusion, Shukri finally realized that

she was indeed in love with Dahabo. It took a while for her to be able to say that she is a lesbian, but that was a step in the right direction, especially since she came from a very traditional background.

Today, the women work together and live together. Shukri has long since accepted her sexuality and the women plan to leave their job in four years, hoping to go to Somalia and start a more permanent life together.

"It has been a long road for me," says Dahabo, who had always hoped to find the right woman, "I'm happy with where I am today. I can see a good future, for the both of us. I can't wait to be with her back in our home country."

They plan to build their own home near a beach in Mogadishu. They will invest in Dahabo's younger brother, who she will have go back and forth between Mogadishu and Dubai, and the couple expect to have more time to relax.

In the meantime, Dahabo and Shukri are trying to stay safe in a country where you can literally be killed for same-sex sexual activities. As such, they keep to themselves and don't even interact much with the queer community in their city.

"We are close to our goal," says Dahabo, with a smile, as they break their fast a few minutes after sunset, "We have to stay safe."

Dubai

Qorax was only sixteen when he was brought to Dubai, to help his uncle run a fabric business. The uncle had moved to Dubai years earlier, and was having a hard time running the business on his own. As a traditional man, and especially being one from the Somali community of Ogadenia in Ethiopia, the uncle did not want to trust anyone but family.

It was in the mid 1980s and it was before Dubai had become the Las Vegas of the Middle East. Things were much simpler back then, and business was becoming more and more plenty.

"I remember it as a nice town," says Qorax, now in his mid forties, having a glass of red wine in a lounge in the Marina area. "This very area we are at, it wasn't even here. There was nothing here."

There might have been nothing here in the mid 1980s, but the Marina is bustling today. It is hip, it is luxurious, and it is everything that is the new Middle East. The atmosphere at this lounge, which has a relaxed ambiance with its nice Brazilian jazz in the background, international staff, and imported wines, it leaves you feeling like you could be anywhere.

"That is exactly the success of Dubai," says Qorax. "It is like the casinos of Las Vegas, without a clock [on the wall] you will never be reminded of the awfulness of time. Similarly, in Dubai, you're hardly ever reminded of being a foreigner. Almost everyone is a foreigner here."

With about 85% foreigners, mostly from Asia and Africa, it is not very difficult to understand how an Emirate with such a large majority of foreigners could rise to the top of the economical ladder and fall just as low, and climb back again. While most people here take their wealth back to their home countries, they still have to work to make that wealth here in the first place, which puts Dubai at an interesting advantage.

There are all kinds of people here, including a large and visible LGBT community. They're on television, at executive levels of the five-star hotels, in the royal families, everywhere. A lot of them are also migrants from other Arab countries, especially people in the entertainment industry who generally keep a second home in Dubai—far from their conservative societies back home.

The foreigner community is not always dreaming of staying, says Qorax.

"Dubai is like the caravan of the past," he explains. "People come here to do business, from the maids to the owners of multi-billion dollar companies," he adds, showing me statistics from a newspaper. "But hardly anyone keeps their money here. Of course, there are the few to whom Dubai is home, and who keep their souls and their money here. Eventually, however, people think they will go somewhere else."

Qorax is one of these people who belong to this city. In 1999, his uncle died, leaving the entire business in the hands of the young man. The uncle, who had left no children as he was never married, made Qorax a legal owner of the business several years before his death—in order to keep the rest of the family from breaking it down in inheritance.

"By that time, we already brought two more of the family," says Qorax. "But they didn't want to work with me, and left the business to start their own businesses. I also know it was because of homophobia; they didn't want a gay man to be their boss."

So, Qorax got smart. As a gay man he knew many gays in Dubai, some from his home area. Slowly, he collected all the gays he knew from his home area in Dubai and neighboring Emirates in the UAE, as well as other countries like Oman, Qatar, and Saudi Arabia.

"Some of these guys were prostitutes, some were business owners, they were very diverse," recalls Qorax, who gave everyone the same chance. "But I wanted to create a gay-run business, because I think we are very good at these things," he laughs.

On top of his Somali businesses, which now have grown to four large companies, Qorax is also now a silent partner in a multi-national company that operates in seven countries in the Middle East.

He credits most of his success to his uncle. I ask the obvious question of whether his uncle was also gay.

"It is something I had been suspecting most of my life," says Qorax, who gets teary-eyed talking about his beloved uncle. "I guess I will never know. I was too stupid to never have come out to him, because I know even if he wasn't he would have accepted me. I know for a fact he knew about me, but it was never official, you know?"

When he was twenty-six, despite his uncle's reservations, Qorax agreed to a marriage arranged by his mother. He is an only child, and his mother, who lost her husband at a young age and who never remarried, said she didn't want to die without a grandchild. He had to go back to Jigjigga, the city of his birth, in order to consummate the marriage.

"I was honest with the woman from the first day we talked on the phone," says Qorax. "She agreed to get married because she believed she had as much to gain as I were. She knew if I turned down the marriage that her father would give her away to the man he wanted her to go with in the first place, which was a friend of his who was three times her age."

The two got married, and he brought the woman to Dubai. She produced one child, and they got divorced. Today, she is married to a man of her choice, and she is happier than she would have been with that old man, says Qorax.

His mother had moved to Dubai and is now living with her son, and enjoys raising her grandson. Before she moved to Dubai, Qorax had come out to her and, even though they don't talk about it, she seems to have made peace with it.

"So, somehow, we all got what we wanted," he says. "I'm good friends with my ex wife, and we have a bond that is much stronger than married people, I think. Her husband knows I'm gay, but he says he is still jealous of me," he laughs.

It seems in Dubai all things are possible.

Mumbai

Mumbai, which changed its name from Bombay to Mumbai in the late 1980s, is a massive metropolis that defies logic. Dharavi, one of the largest slums in the world, is only a couple of miles away from the luxurious residences of the Bollywood stars in Bandra.

"It is a city of contradictions," says Kamal, a 26-year-old gay Somali who lives here. "For example, it is a very developed city, there are skyscrapers and everything, but nobody really knows what the number of the population really is," he laughs. "This is Mumbai."

Five years ago, at the age of 21, Kamal won a scholarship to a university in Pakistan. He was going to study, and then was planning to go back to Berbera and put that education to good use.

But, life had other plans for the young man; within just mere weeks of arriving at the university he met another student and fell in love.

"I just knew I wanted to be with him," says Kamal, who at the time never had the experience to fall in love. "Everything I ever imagined I found in him, and I thought that was it."

Well, it was "it" for two years. They had a blissful time. However, when the family of the other young man discovered about the relationship, he was immediately put into an arranged marriage.

"I was heartbroken," says Kamal, whose partner stopped contact overnight. "I couldn't stay in Pakistan, but

I didn't want to go back home, either. So, I decided to come to India."

Here, he met a young man he knew from his university days in Pakistan, who had graduated the year before and who made a life for himself in Mumbai.

The problem was that Kamal never really understood exactly what the young man was doing in Mumbai.

"He would say he was in business," remembers Kamal, laughing, "I just never got the particulars of what type of business he was in. He was always so mysterious about it."

The young man was a high-class escort, working for a group of older men who were running luxury apartments full of sexy guys whose bodies they were renting out for a fee to the wealthy and the elite.

He had spoken about Kamal to his pimps, selling him as a sexy "African and Arab" mix whom the Pakistanis had the hots for, arguing that he would be successful in Mumbai as an escort.

Kamal, of course, needed to be healed. He was given about six months to get over his heartache, and at the same time was assigned a personal trainer who was going to shape his body into escort-ready physique.

"By that time, I really was ready," he says, laughing, "I was broke and I was living with all these guys who were making a lot of money. I was ready, indeed!"

His pimps put him to work, and Kamal began to make a lot of money. The more he made, the more he was getting addicted to the lifestyle. He was living in a five-star condo, with servants seeing to all of his needs, and he had the money to enjoy a city that offers a decadent experience to those who can afford it.

But Kamal's life is a window into another contradiction of Mumbai. While Kamal is part of an organized community, utilizing the Internet and their personal connections to attract wealthy and powerful clientele, a large number of male prostitutes in Mumbai are living in a different reality. They are working for next to nothing, and often times their lives are in danger. When they are not in constant danger of being arrested by the police, their customers might abuse them or even kill them.

On many gay websites, you find some of these Mumbaikar escorts who are working for ten to fifty dollars—going to hotel rooms and homes of men they don't know, many of them married, and some of them psychologically disturbed.

On the other hand, elite escorts like Kamal can end up making thousands of dollars per night. If he were to go on a long weekend to Dubai or to Muscat, he ends up making tens of thousands of dollars.

The stark difference between the two groups is incredible, and Kamal says it speaks more about the larger culture than it does about the abilities of individuals.

"This is a culture that affords some opportunities to some people," says Kamal. "In Berbera you cannot yell at a taxi driver just because he is a taxi driver, because he could come from just as powerful of a tribe as you do, but in Karachi and Mumbai you can perfectly yell at a taxi driver and he will lower his gaze, especially if you happen to come from a certain background."

It is not just about castes and class, however, in a city like Mumbai. It is also about age and vanity. Kamal knows his days of being considered "hot" are numbered. When he reaches in his thirties he will have to either retire from the business completely or change his position in it.

"I'm saving money, and I plan to start a normal business," Kamal replies when I ask him if he has thought about what he will do. "This business is vicious. Under all the luxuries, this is really a bad business. There are days when I feel like I want to quit and go somewhere else."

But he doesn't, because for now it works. He is able to save money, and he is also able to make the living conditions of the people he loves back home a bit easier.

"Now I'm the one who says I'm in business to people," he laughs, telling me he sends money back home with the family thinking he is working in a company with his education. "But someday soon, I hope, I will be able to say that and not feel like a liar."

Kamal is currently enrolled in an online school, studying Information Technology. He doesn't want to go back to his country. Instead, he wants to move to Bangalore and start his own Internet-based business.

He is also moving to Bangalore because he had met a man there a year ago. They have been meeting, traveling back and forth, and the man doesn't know what Kamal does for a living, but Kamal hopes to be closer to him.

"I'm giving this business another year or two," he says, "Then I'm out."

Kamal had already reinvented himself before, from a brokenhearted student to a high-class escort, and he says he is confident to be able to reinvent himself in Bangalore.

I have no doubt.

Oslo

One Sunday morning, as most people woke up to their peaceful day, Amal Aden woke up to find 146 threatening voicemails and text messages on her phone. Why? Because she attended the gay pride parade in Oslo as an openly lesbian Muslim, and many people in the community felt that she was not a good role model to the Muslim children.

"I'm lesbian, Muslim and Somali—it is not a simple combination," she wrote in a local newspaper in Norwegian. "It can be difficult for ethnic Norwegians to understand how difficult and painful it can be to be both Muslim and for gay rights."

Many years ago Amal came out of the closet as a lesbian. She was covered in the media all over Europe, she wrote several books, and has had many experiences of encountering homophobia both in the Somali and larger Muslim community.

"People have spit at me, thrown things at me, and threatened to kill me," she told *The Local*. Amal, who while proud of her sexuality is also mindful of how other people are looking at her life, adds "I've spent many nights awake in despair over how my sexual orientation could create so much hatred."

Norway is very much the European Union model. It is a country that celebrates its diversity, and has been on the forefront in the fight for LGBT Rights. For the pride parade attended by Amal, the city's mayor was joined by the country's cultural and developmental ministers in making sure LGBT people felt important, included, and protected.

"Of course, that doesn't mean the Norwegian government can control what people believe," says Hadiyo Jim'ale, the leader of the LGBT Somali organization called *Queer Somalis*. "However, when there have been cases of verbal and physical abuse the government then does act and does its job in protecting LGBT people."

Ubaydullah Hussain, a controversial Islamist and former football referee, is one of many who have been prosecuted for hate speech. He verbally attacked Amal for her sexual orientation. He was handed a 120-day prison sentence.

Section 135a of Norway's legal statutes prohibits public expressions that are hateful or discriminating. Because free speech is a very important part of the country's values, it had been often difficult in the past to challenge people under this law. However, some recent Norwegian Supreme Court rulings have aided the authorities in prosecuting people like Ubaydullah Hussain.

"I was so happy when that guy was convicted," said Rashid, a young gay Somali who left his hometown of Bergen for fear his family would hurt him. "We need more people like Amal, who are willing to stand up for our identities and our rights," he added, showing a picture of his Somali ex-boyfriend, who broke up with Rashid because he couldn't reconcile the Somali culture and his sexuality. "We need to change this."

Rashid did mention there are a lot of things changing in the community, especially as more and more people come forward. For example, a few years ago he saw Imam Daayiee Abdullah on television. The experience changed the young man's life.

"The lovely Imam Daayiee said being gay and Muslim is okay," says Rashid, whose family immigrated to Norway when he was a child, escaping the civil war in Somalia. "It was so nice to hear those words from an imam. I felt so liberated by his words, and his attitude gave me the reassurance I needed."

Although Imam Daayiee, who is one of the few spiritual leaders in the Muslim community that are openly gay, has been in Norway several times, appeared in various television programs, and has worked with local organizations, and contributed greatly to the discussion on the subject, young people in Norway still need to see other Norwegians come forward.

"That is why Amal is so important to me," says Farha, a lesbian of Paksitani background. "We need to see more Muslims like her to challenge the local community here. It was because of her I was able to talk to my parents, and explain my life to them in ways I didn't think I could before I knew about her."

Amal was born in Somalia in 1983. Following the 1991 civil war, the young Amal was living in fear, lonely, and hungry. She came to Norway in 1996, and completely changed her life. She got educated, and opened her eyes to the freedoms in Europe.

Then, in 2008 Amal's book came out. The book, entitled "Se oss!" ("Sees Us"), was critical of the Somali community in Norway and what she called the enabling social welfare system of the country. As an openly lesbian, and one of the few in the Muslim community, her work has encountered a lot of controversy and one time had to be living in hiding.

Today, she is one of the well-respected people in the country. She often goes around lecturing and talking about her life. The queer community, both Somali and non-Somali, have recognized her contribution to the conversation about sexuality in the communities.

Paris

Jamal was born in a suburb outside of Paris. His parents are Somalis from Djibouti, and they met in a university in the United Kingdom and later moved to France.

He was born in a neighborhood full of French kids from various backgrounds. Most of the families here are North African, especially Algerian. But a lot of them are also from West African backgrounds.

"Of course, I don't fit with either group, in terms of the way I look," he laughs, showing me a picture of him with his friends as a young boy; two of whom I guessed to have North African background and three of West African. "They always called me *métis*, to make fun of me," he adds, talking about a term used in France to refer to people who are mixed race. "But I love these guys! They're my family, closer than my own siblings!"

Jamal is a very interesting character. He came out to his buddies when he was 11. What is so cool about his story is that they immediately accepted him. No one made fun of him for his sexuality. Perhaps he was always the strongest, as he still seems physically larger than the rest.

"It was his character," remembers Mamadou, whose parents came from Benin when he was just a month old. "He was always a happy guy, and we liked him. It didn't matter what or who he was sexually."

Karim, whose grandparents came to France in the 1950s from Morocco, says it wasn't always easy for him in the group, but that overall things were good between them.

"Of course, we made fun of him sometimes," says Cheik, whose parents moved to France from Senegal in the 1970s. "If you were angry with him you called him a faggot, and he gave you the finger."

Jamal says he was not singled out. Everyone was called derogatory names, but that none of them ever took it seriously. They fought, as all friends, but they always knew they cared about each other.

When he came out to his parents, however, at age eighteen, it was a little different. They didn't take the news so easily, because they had been planning on sending him to Djibouti after his studies.

"They were disappointed," he says. "They loved me, but they asked me to try and change. I told them I was not going to do that, and they were really offended, thinking I was taking the matter easily. We had some fights, and we didn't speak for a few years," he adds, saying it was his patience that paid off. "Eventually, they started to understand I was not doing this to belittle them or our culture."

In the meantime, he got a great job in Paris and moved to the center. He is still very much involved in the lives of his childhood friends, and they are all still in each other's lives.

"I'm with these guys forever," he laughs. "They are closer to me than any boyfriend. All of their girlfriends know they will leave them if I say so," he adds, pointing fingers at two of them, as we eat couscous in a Moroccan restaurant.

As was the last several years, his friends join him in the gay pride march. They bring their girlfriends, and two of them even bring their kids along. It is really a nice scene of friendship, respect, and love.

At one point, during the march, a friendly woman looks at Jamal and tells him, "Go back to Africa!"

But Jamal smiles, and barks back, "I'm from Paris, bitch!"

She smiles.

Jamal lives a very Parisian life. Monday to Friday he is in Paris, working. He owns a little apartment in the north-western part of town, in the 17th District, a few blocks from the busy Place de Clichy.

He works in La Défense, Europe's largest purpose-built business district, which is a thirty-minute train commute from his apartment.

Most evenings, he is busy attending exhibitions or watching foreign movies at theaters. His calendar is filled with events, and he says he would do more if he could.

Then there is Michel, his part time lover. Michel is in an open relationship, and can only meet Jamal twice or three times per week.

"It works for me, honestly," he laughs, "I'm very busy and that is all I can handle," he adds.

On the weekends, he is back in his childhood neighbor-hood in the suburbs. He meets his family and friends, and he is happy.

London

It is an unusually warm Saturday afternoon in November—a treasure in London. And weather-savvy Londoners like Dylan know not to miss the opportunity to put such days to good use. He has good plans for the day. And if his five o'clock workout that morning was any indication, it will be a day fostered by outdoor activities.

Standing at a Bayswater Road bus stop, Hyde Park giving its blissful dose of fresh air in the background, Dylan, a twenty-six year old gay man, is busy reading a tabloid magazine. He seems to be lost in the pages; his eyes flickering left and right—assumedly shocked by the latest celebrity gossip.

"Such rubbish," he says out loud.

I get curious about what he is reading.

"It is about Madonna," he says, rather disappointedly.

Madonna is Dylan's idol. Ever since he was a child, he loved the American pop star. He begged his parents to buy him tickets to her concerts for years. They wouldn't let him. When he was seventeen he had the chance to buy it himself—and that was only after working at his uncle's shop on the weekends for many months.

"She has a love-hate relationship with the British press," he says.

Today, he is reading about gossip pertaining to her adoption from Malawi. Madonna has been accused in the papers of using the adoption as a way to get publicity, something Dylan says the pop star has been accused of throughout her career—doing shocking things just to get press, that is.

"But really," he says, in her defense, "Madonna is a such a good person!"

When he sees he convinced me, he drifts back to the pages.

Dylan looks up when his concentration is suddenly interrupted by the arrival of the 148 bus, which is headed to Marble Arch. After a few of the riders get off, a tall and rather handsome Somali man jumps out.

Dylan smiles.

"Here comes Mo," he says.

The two hug and kiss on the lips.

Dylan whispers something to Mo.

"I love you, too," whispers Mo, into Dylan's ear.

Dylan smiles again, as they drift off together in the park.

Seven years earlier, Dylan met Mo at Heathrow Airport. At the time, Dylan worked as a Security Guard there. His responsibility was to screen travelers. During a regular work break, he was in a bathroom when another young man motioned for him to join him in a stall, which left the young British utterly conflicted.

"I didn't dare to go there," says Dylan. "But I was also madly attracted."

Dylan was only nineteen at the time, and had no previous experience of the sort. And although he had attraction towards other men before, he never acted on it. So having sex in public was not something he even thought about.

After Mo persisted, Dylan gave in.

"It was perfect," he says. "Then he told me, of course."

Mo had been living in the airport for days. He didn't know anyone in London. He had no money as one of his bags, in which he had his money, was lost or stolen. And he knew if he left the airport, he could have ended up on the streets. At least at the airport, figured Mo, it was warm.

"I could pretend to be any traveler," says Mo. "I could sleep there, and no one would question me because people didn't even stop to think about it. They just assumed I was waiting for a flight. A lot of people were sleeping there because some flights had been delayed or canceled due to the weather conditions of their destinations."

I wondered why he didn't talk to Somali people, especially since there are a lot of Somalis working in the airport.

"Because I didn't want people to ask me what tribe I belong to," says Mo. "I knew if they knew who I was they could find my relatives and I could end up having to live with them. I didn't want to live with Somalis."

He begged Dylan to let him stay with him.

"I didn't know what to say," says Dylan. "So I took him home with me."

Dylan says he made it clear to Mo that he could only promise to give him shelter for the night. At the time, Dylan was living with four other guys his age. They were all sharing a two-bedroom flat in West London. Dylan and his roommates, all from a suburb outside of London where they grew up together, were lifelong friends. They were all from middle class white families. Bringing in an African immigrant was not exactly something they had discussed beforehand.

The roommates were polite enough to let the poor guy stay for the night, but when Dylan came out to tell them he had wishes of Mohammed staying longer, well, let's just say it created a little rift amongst them.

"I wasn't quite ready to tell them about my sexual relationship with Mo," says Dylan. "So they didn't understand why I wanted him to live with us. They accused him of being a user, and even said he could end up stealing from all of us. It was tough."

Suddenly, Dylan's world became a bit complicated. It turned out that Mo had no proper papers to stay in the country. He was illegal. Dylan was risking his freedom—not to mention the freedom of his friends—by harboring an illegal immigrant.

"I was torn to pieces," says Dylan. "But there was no doubt I wanted to help."

Dylan didn't have the means to hire a lawyer. He had no way to find support to help Mo. He couldn't talk to his family unless he was willing to come out, which he wasn't ready for at that moment in time. He was smart to talk to a friend of his from work. The friend, from Nigeria, pointed him to a lot of different organizations that helped people like Mo resettle in the United Kingdom.

"But I didn't have experience with this sort of thing," admits Dylan. "It took me quite a bit of time to weave through the immigration jargons to actually understand how exactly Mo was seen in Britain. I didn't know what exactly asylum meant."

Mo filed for asylum because his family in Somalia had tried to force him to get married. When he refused to go through with the arrangement on the day of the wedding, after an awful panic, and admitted to his homosexuality, the family vowed to kill him unless he repented and did what was expected of him.

"They were not joking," says Mo. "They were serious."

Mo, who was twenty-two at that time, was the oldest son and therefore in control of the family business, which included two stores in a main market and six passenger-carrying buses. When he realized the danger he was in he secretly sold the buses to a local rival, took the money and headed for anywhere outside his country.

"It didn't matter where I went," he says. "But I wanted to go to London."

I was curious to know how Mo was able to come to London.

"I came in legally, sort of," Mo says. "I left Mogadishu and smuggled my way to Nairobi, Kenya. Then I paid five thousand USD to a Somali man who is a famous smuggler there. He got me a Kenyan passport with visa on it. Of course, it was not real. And to avoid my being returned to Kenya, which then would mean he would have to pay me back half of the money, he instructed me to destroy all the documents once I got to London. He also instructed me not say what country I had directly come from. I was to say I was from Somalia, and that is it."

It would be two years before Mo was legal. At the time Somalia did not have functioning government. There was no way to return Somali citizens to their countries. And while Dylan knew Mo would ultimately become legal, based on the advice he was getting from organizations, the process was very stressful experience for the both of them.

"My biggest problem was money," says Dylan. "I was making just enough to survive, Mo was not able to help anyhow, and the everyday expenses like paying the bus fare to go to an immigration office was become huge. And I think I was taking a bit of that stress on Mo and our relationship."

By the time Mo became legal, the couple had lost their way with one another. They no longer made love. And when they did make love, says Dylan, it was not something enjoyable. There wasn't any passion left.

So they broke up.

"But we stayed friends," says Dylan.

A year later, they slowly found their way back and they are together ever since.

"I guess what I learned the most out of that experience is that love is not something that can be planned," says Dylan. "We don't know who we are going to meet. Regardless of the circumstances, Mo and I are very grateful we found each other. We realized we have to grab love wherever it finds us."

And grab they did.

Over the past few years, Dylan and Mo found ways to

make peace with their lives. For Dylan, he was able to go to university, accept his homosexuality and even came out to his parents. He expected the worst with the parents, as feared their rejection, but they surprised him when they said they had known all along and had accepted it.

"It is quite nice, actually," says Dylan. "It is certainly far cry from what I thought my life would be like in my twenties. I was such an unhappy child growing up. And really I thought that would be my life. But now I'm happy. I'm really happy. I never want to think about what my life would have been like without him."

For Mo, he finally is in touch with his family again. He says they are not thrilled about his life as a gay man but they are making progress. In London he found relatives who are willing to accept him, much better than those back home, because of the western influence here. One of his close friends now is a cousin.

"I have been thinking about Somalia a lot lately," says Mo. "I try to imagine what my life would have been like had I married that girl and was living a life I didn't want. It is painful to think there are thousands in that situation in my country. I really don't know why I was spared, but I'm glad I was spared."

Today, it is their seventh year anniversary (they count from that fateful afternoon at the airport). As usual, they are having a party at Dylan's parents' house. Many friends and family are expected. But that is much later in the day. As usual, they will want to spend sometime with one another before that.

"He brought this," says Dylan, showing me *xalwad*, a

Somali sweet often used to celebrate weddings, which is why Mo had to go to East London earlier that morning. "He says this is how it is done in the old country. Really, I just think he wants me to get fat is all, don't you think?"

Mo stuffs more sweets into Dylan's mouth, as to stop him from talking. In response Dylan kisses him, and Mo has some of that sweet on his upper lip now. And so goes one more romantic moment in Hyde Park.

Geneva

By the time I came to America in my teens, I had met at least a dozen queer Somalis—all of them men; I had yet to meet a lesbian. The word used for lesbian in Somali, *qaniisad*, is the feminine version of the word *qaniis* or gay.

A few years later, I finally met a *qaniisad*. Her name was Rahma and she visiting from Switzerland. She was a 25-year-old student and *nin-nin*, or masculine, in terms of behavior. But, at the same time, she possessed lots of feminine qualities like long hair, pretty nails and wore the fabulous *dirac*, the see-through kind.

Normally, the dirac went all the way below a woman's feet, which then the woman would grab with one hand and would hold onto while walking, part of her *xarago*, her beauty. The holding was generally necessary, because as you held onto it you could change your walking strategies. Hence, you could walk fast, sexy, or however you wanted.

Being masculine, however, Rahma had her dirac supported by her *goorgarad*, a beautiful and shiny inner skirt that is silky and a different color from the dirac, accompanied by a *rejistiin*, a bra of the same color as the goorgarad. Instead of holding it, she just tucked part of the front under the goorgarad.

When I was in Somalia, I used to see a lot of women do that with their dress. Then I asked Rahma whether that was a clue to their sexuality or not.

"No, honey," she said, laughing. "It is actually common for women to do this when they want to use both of their hands. I'm just a dyke and can't drag a dress all day."

In Somali culture, women encourage themselves to drag it because they believe in the idea of *xarago xanuunkeed* or "beauty has its pains." They use the same proverb when justifying wearing painfully tall high-heels.

Rahma, on the other hand, is wearing medium-high open shoes and actually seems to be comfortable.

"Why bother? Shoes are just shoes," she protested, and with which I agreed. "They are meant to complement your clothes, not to put you in pain," she added, "I don't understand that thinking."

Rahma is beautiful, indeed, but her beauty gets even deeper when she talks about queer issues. She is passionate about LGBT Rights, especially since she believes one of the women of a lesbian couple that was executed in Somalia was her ex.

A few years before Rama and I met a story broke out to the international community that the women were executed in a northeastern region of Somalia, which had declared itself autonomous and named itself "Puntland."

Rahma said she was scared for Somali lesbians, in general, but then she received a word from Somalia that one of the victims was her ex-girlfriend.

"A lesbian called me in the middle of the night," says Rahma. "It was a horrible news because my ex-girlfriend and I did not break up because the relationship died but because of the war. We got separated and then her family married her off to some guy."

When the civil war broke out Rahma's family went to Kenya, and she eventually ended up in Europe. In the meantime, her ex's family went to their ancestral home area of Burco, a city that was then part of the western region of Waqooyi in Somalia but is now part of the autonomous "Somaliland."

Rahma tried to find out everything she could about the executed couple, but Putland denied it. She says she contacted at least three different people in that region and they confirmed the story was actually true.

The executed women, who belonged to the Majeerteen and Isaaq clans, were executed "discreetly."

Rahma, who is an Isaaq herself and whose ex was also Isaaq, is not sure how her ex got to Puntland, which is generally not normal, as they are two different countries these days and inhabited by two different tribes. She tried to contact her ex's family, but she hasn't been successful in finding them, she says.

Rahma came to Europe in 1991 when she got into Italy illegally. A lot of Somali women were doing the same thing. Italy was "big" with the women because you could become *booyaaso* or a maid, says Rahma.

Afterwards she went into Switzerland and filed for asylum as a refugee.

"Coming to Switzerland was the best thing I did," says Rahma, who moved to a region in Switzerland that speaks French. "I could go to school and envision a good life. I learned a new language, and I could change my life."

Change is exactly what she did. She went to school and now she is almost done with her medical school. What is she going to be?

"A gynecologist," she says. "I want to help Somali girls understand their bodies and deal with some of the things they are faced with, some of the things we don't talk about, and some of the things they need to change with their own daughters in the future."

Rahma is a fierce feminist. She had been going to communities all over Switzerland, teaching Somali women sobering facts about a very extreme female circumcision, which is known to us as *gudniinka fircooniga* and known to others as Female Genital Mutilation (FGM).

"The education on this horrible practice is very low within the Somali community," she says to Somali women in a community gathering outside of Geneva. "Women, especially, need to empower themselves by studying the cases. There is enough information on this out there for anyone who is interested. Please, for the sake of your daughters, stop this practice."

Like most Somali girls Rahma suffered the practice, which she says most Somalis do in order to keep the girls' sexuality 'under control.'

"By cutting down the pleasure the girls will not sin by having premarital sex," she explains the reasoning behind it. "It is of course all for men. It is a tactic to keep women virgins until they marry."

But because of that many of these victims of FGM end up hating their bodies, and men, as sex and menstruation become painful experiences for the young women.

Fortunately, Rahma is not one of them. In 2003, for an interview with *Huriyah* magazine, when asked what she thinks of her vagina, she had talked about her body in a positive manner.

"I love my vagina," she told us then. "When the civil war started, I would have gone crazy without satisfying myself, after my girlfriend left me and moved with her family to the other side of the country. It saved my life, literally."

I can't help but be proud of her, both as a Somali and queer. It is nice to hear a Somali woman talking about her body and her sexuality in a manner that is devoid of shame, devoid of all that had been forced on our women.

So, what is she doing now?

"Enjoying my life with my girlfriend," she says. "I'm looking forward to becoming a doctor, as well. My life is in good shape. I didn't write it this way but I absolutely love it. My girlfriend and I have made definite plans for a marriage."

What a sweet life.

Toronto

Dahir was born and raised in Mogadishu. He was born in the late 1980s, and by the time the civil war took place he was only a child. Chaos, uncertainty, and bloodshed—these are all of the things the children of Somalia grew up with in their country in the 1990s.

But that wasn't all Dahir had to deal with.

"I'm gay," he says. "I'm a sissy boy, and therefore automatically openly gay."

This was the reason, he believes, that his father approached him with marriage at age seventeen, to a cousin. Knowing he was gay, and knowing what it could mean for his innocent cousin, Dahir declined.

"I told my father that she was like my sister," Dahir remembers. "He agreed, but he had his conditions. I had to find another woman of my choice to marry, and as soon as possible."

This prompted him to leave the country. He went to Yemen by boat. He lived there for six months. He found work at a car wash, and was met with homophobia. He was bullied to the point of leaving the job.

"Knowing getting another job would be next to impossible, I decided to go and try my luck in Saudi Arabia," Dahir recounts. "Unfortunately, the Saudis arrested me at the border and immediately deported me back to Somalia."

For this story I read a report by Human Rights Watch that said around 12,000 Somalis were deported from Saudi Arabia in 2014. The organization argued that Saudi Arabia should end the "summary deportations, which risk violating its international obligations not to return anyone to a place where their life or freedom is threatened or where they face other serious harm."

It is not just Somalis. According to the International Business Times there were around 1 million people who were deported from Saudi Arabia in 2014, and that the majority of the immigrants in the country are Asian.

When Dahir was deported back to Somalia in 2004, as luck would have it, his father was out of town on business. His mother, worried for her son's safety, urged him to leave town before the father returned.

"She gave me transport money, and sent me to her sister in Kenya," says Dahir.

Dahir jumped at the chance. He blossomed in Kenya, understanding his sexuality further and becoming more involved in the gay communities online and offline. He lived there for four years until the unemployment became too much for him.

In 2008 his paternal aunt called him to South Africa. She owned a business there and said she was in need of family to help her run it. Dahir accepted the proposal immediately, and moved to Cape Town.

In South Africa Dahir was urged to be careful. He found out that the Somali community had been facing a lot of discrimination. Many Somali businesses were looted, and some Somali business people were beaten, injured, and even killed.

After working for his aunt for some time, which was

not his first choice, Dahir decided to go into business with some friends of his. They opened a shop in Khayelitsha, a township just outside of Cape Town. Some South African business owners in the area were unhappy with them, and warned them to leave.

"We didn't heed their warning," says Dahir. "Our business was looted and I was beaten very badly by eight strong men. My business partner was shot in the stomach. He had to undergo surgery to save his life."

Without income, and not being able to get a job, Dahir went back to his aunt. As they saw his gay friends visit him, the family began to have problems with Dahir. He began fighting with his homophobic cousins, and he was told to leave.

At that point Dahir says he became very depressed. He began to think perhaps everyone else was right and thought about ways to change what he perceived to be the problem—not just his sexuality but his lifestyle altogether.

"I was tired of running," says Dahir. "I was just tired. I wanted to change my life. I decided to become what people wanted me to become. I cut my long hair, I took off my earrings, and I put on a white *qamiis* to be a good Muslim."

He moved to Johannesburg, a city he knew no one would know his face. He found a job there with a religious Somali man. The man had just opened his store and promised he would pay Dahir later. Instead the man began to only pay him fraction of the salary so he could barely live.

"Then people I knew from Cape Town came to Johannesburg," remembers Dahir. "They told my boss to fire me because I was a faggot and he shouldn't employ faggots. He fired me, and didn't pay me my salary."

His gay friends from Cape Town told him to report the case to the Commissioner for Conciliation, Mediation and Arbitration (CCMA), which is a dispute resolution body established through the Labour Relations Act of 1995. Dahir filed a case with the CCMA and his boss was summoned.

"My boss tricked me," says Dahir. "He told me he would pay me and re-employ me if I withdrew the case. I did it only after he signed a settlement, but he decided against it anyway and refused to pay me. The CCMA told me there was nothing they could do as I withdrew the case."

Once more, in his fourth country, Dahir's sexuality was becoming a problem. His former boss told everyone that Dahir was gay and no one should employ him. No one employed him. He became homeless and was sleeping in a Methodist church with a lot of other refugees.

"With the refugees I learned about a Canadian office in downtown," says Dahir. "I was happy and I immediately went to their office. They helped me with one month's rent, and opened a resettlement case for me."

He couldn't stay in Johannesburg and went back to Cape Town. However, he continued with his Canadian case in Cape Town. In the meantime he got a job at a restaurant as a dishwasher, and life became a bit better.

"It wasn't much, the money," says Dahir, "But I was able to live my life. I was able to rent my own room, and I became happy again. It was so nice to finally be able to be myself. To be whole again. To be able to do the things I wanted to do."

Years later, in the middle of 2013, the Canadians called. His case was approved. The process went pretty fast after that and soon he was in Canada.

Today Dahir lives in Toronto. His dream is to finish the Level 7 ESL, go to college, and become a working professional.

"I'm so happy to be in Canada," says Dahir. "Life has completely changed for me. I'm in the best country in the world."

Seattle

"Oh, it is beautiful being a *gabadh* [girl]," says Hamdi, a Somali trans woman who now lives in Seattle. "Somali men treat you better. I really enjoy my days as a woman better than when I was a guy."

Hamdi, who has gone through a gender reassignment surgery, was born a male. The proud parents named the boy Sa'id. Later, she named herself Hamdi, an Arabic name that translates to "being thankful," when she moved to a new community that was more accepting.

"The name goes with how I felt. I was thankful to be who I was. It just came to me one night, and in the morning I told everyone I wanted to be called that name."

As a boy Hamdi says she thought she was gay, but she also knew there was something different about the way she felt about other boys.

"I wasn't just another boy," she says. "I was a girl inside a boy's body. This was very confusing to a teen who did not even know there was such thing as a transsexual."

She even once told a boyfriend, after he fell in love with her, that she had always felt she was a girl inside.

"He freaked out. I remember he was shaking and was trying not to touch me. He was gay and I just told him I was a woman, how would anyone feel? It was a shock. Anyway, one night he tried to kill me."

There was something psychologically wrong with him, believes Hamdi, who says her boyfriend was always a little temperamental but that the later months of their relationship he turned totally violent. They were fighting a lot, and he would physically attack her. One night, she had returned to her family after a wedding and found him sitting in her room with a knife.

"He said he was going to murder me."

Her brothers sent the guy home that night, but Hamdi knew it was over with him and that she couldn't stay where she was.

Hamdi, who at the time lived and is originally from the northern Somali state of Waqooyi, ran away after that incident to Mogadishu, the southern capital.

"I packed my bags and boarded on a bus the next morning," she recalls. "Next stop, Hamar [Mogadishu]. That was one of the wildest things I have ever done. I was scared. Fear makes you do all sorts of strange things."

In Mogadishu she found communities in which, she was told, she could live as gay or as anything else she wanted to be and would be accepted.

"It was like a dream come true for me," says the now 29-year-old woman, who became a nurse after she had moved to the U.S. in the mid 1990s. "I immediately moved to Hamar-Jajab [a district in Mogadishu.] It wasn't easy having to find a place to live and work, but it was the best thing that I have ever done for myself."

Hamdi says she found the community there to be exactly what she was looking for; gay men wearing women's clothing.

"I thought 'this is it.'"

As time went on, a whole village of gay men dressed like women became a bit too much for the well-dressed tall Hamdi.

"Suddenly, the reality hit," she says, polishing her nails as she sighs. "I was confronted with an entire district that was like me. Even though it was very nice to be accepted, I had realized I was one of the lucky ones there. Not everything seemed as rosy."

Soon, she found out that those gay men who did not want to dress like women were not welcome.

In fact, she says, "they were chased away from the neighborhood whenever they came around there to pick up drag queens. It was horrible. I was not attracted to drag queens, I was attracted to men who dressed like men," she recounts, sadly. "But I was not allowed to be with them. No, you had to punish them and chase them away. It was very strange."

Because she was young and broke, and Hamdi was smart enough to realize she had to put up with whatever rules she was told to follow. But she met straight men on the side and was able to carry out love affairs with the kinds of men she wanted.

"I had to sneak around," she remembers, laughing infectiously, "but I definitely broke all the rules. I was a rebel!"

Many years later, after meeting one of the trans women from that era, Hamdi learned she was actually in a trans compound. It wasn't that gay men were not allowed but that it was a way to protect the compound.

After the civil war broke out in Somalia, Hamdi finally got the freedom she desired. She went to a Kenyan refugee camp outside of Mombasa. Once there, she met others who were in the same situation as her.

"After a few years of making life there, I was able to emigrate to the United States," says Hamdi, who emigrated through a sponsorship by a church. "After that, things eased out for me."

Today, she has no desire for her old roots. Even with fond memories, she fears for her safety and does not wish to go back to her country.

"I think I became too American," she says, playing with her red hair, a color she says she got from applying henna to her hair—although it looks chemically induced color. "It would be foolishness to think I can just go back and everything will be like old times. Everything has changed. The Somali community has changed, and so have I."

A few years after she immigrated to America, Hamdi met a Somali man. The couple met in college and developed a friendship. Without knowing about her gender history, as she doesn't discuss that with people until she knows them very well, the man fell in love with her.

"For the first time in my life, I met someone who loved me completely," she says of the man. "I didn't have the heart to tell him everything. I was scared of losing him. After all, he was a Somali man and God knows about my people and their ideas. I just couldn't do it."

So for years she hid her past. He started to bug her about marriage, which she was not ready for until she told him her secret. A few years ago, when she could no longer keep up the charade and she told him everything.

"He disappeared for nearly a month," she remembers.

Since then, he came back and the two continued their lives—even getting married. Today, a quiet life replaces her traumatic past.

"Life is too short," says Hamdi, "And marriage has been a long dream of mine. And I'm very grateful that it has finally come true."

Minneapolis

He is young. He is black. He is muscular. He is exactly everything that is 'in' today, at least in the gay male community. At the age of 28, although he doesn't really know his exact birthdate, Dadirow is breathtaking.

In a crowded gay bar in Minneapolis' Uptown neighborhood, the gay mecca of the city, I finally meet him.

He is standing tall between two guys and they are both looking at him like they want to eat him right then and there. And many guys around the room are glancing at him.

Part of it, I suspect, has to do with the fact that most gay men in that bar don't see Somali men like him in their everyday lives. His physique is very American, yet he has that typical Somali look.

"No one suspects I'm HIV-positive," he says, smiling with perfect teeth. "And even when I tell them they don't believe me."

He looks very healthy, and he is proud of knowing his status and is not ashamed. When it comes to the Somali community, which has been known to be HIVophobic, he is not exactly the image that comes to mind when people think of the disease.

"Because, honey, I choose to live," he says, pointing his bottle of water at me. "Life is so full of goodness and I choose to not abuse it but take as much as I can, while I give more back to myself."

Six years earlier Dadirow had series of unsafe sex with

147

other gay men in his city. It was a period of depression, and drugs and sex were a good way to deal with it... or so was his thinking at that time.

"It was stupid," he says, sighing. "I thought 'Well, I'm only having sex with people I know are negative.' But that wasn't true because people never tell you everything you need to know."

He doesn't know the identity of the man from whom he contracted the disease. When he found out he was positive he went through the list of people he had been with, but he knows there were many partners he couldn't remember during nights he was too drunk or too high. However, he did do the responsible thing—albeit with a bit of revenge involved—of the lovers he was in touch with.

"I notified all of them my own way," he remembers, laughing. "I sent them e-mails that warned them they would die of slow death."

I didn't meet Dadirow to talk about death, however. I met Dadirow so I could spend a 24-hour period with him to see how he lives his life, and to report on the day of the life of an HIV-positive gay Somali man.

"I will do it," he told me, reluctantly, "I care about people, and so I'm only doing this to help people understand the stigma is not necessary," he adds, much to my delight as he was the sixth HIV-positive man I talked—all the rest refusing to do so, despite the anonymity I promised.

I would come over to his place the night before and would shadow him the following day. He would have to get permission from all those who are in his life—his job, his friends, et cetera.

On the evening I arrived at his place he had already made the guest room for me, which was very simple and chic, decorated with Ikea items but with Somali flair.

"Minneapolis is home to the largest Somali community in the United States," he told me, as we drove around in the south side of the city, going from one Somali shopping mall to the next.

That night, which was a Sunday, we stayed up until eleven, talking about his life. I was fascinated by all of the troubles he had gone through, and how he was able to stay afloat in life and made something of himself.

He survived child abuse, as his father was a drunk in Somalia and would come and beat him and his mother. At age ten he became a refugee in Ethiopia, where his family lived for two years before coming to the United States to join his older sister. Finally, at age seventeen he was kicked out of his family home when the family learned he was gay.

After hearing the awful details of his past I began to see Dadirow differently, and began to have more serious respect for him. At first I thought he was someone too preoccupied with his body. In retrospect I understood he was just living his life, enjoying whatever he could.

The next morning, at five in the morning I wake up because that is the time he wakes up. I watch him take his pills. He doesn't take as many medications as I thought. Only three.

By half past five, we were at the GYM.

"This is my daily contact with my God," he says, pointing his fingers at his torso, which is tight and defined. "My body is my Temple. It gives me 23 hours of blessings each day and it only requires a maintenance that takes no more than an hour a day. Is that so much to ask?"

No, obviously not, I laugh.

By seven, we are back at his place. He takes a shower and we have breakfast. I carefully take account of his. Two egg whites and one-yolk scrambled eggs, a toast, and served with fresh fruit smoothie.

After breakfast, he changes into a suit. We arrive at his job an hour later. He works as a teller supervisor for a busy local bank.

"My day is usually stressful," he notes later around eleven, while he multi-tasks with work and snacking at his desk. "I oversee ten people and a whole lot of money. That is a lot of pressure, so I must keep my energy going," which is why he has a small bowl of fresh grapes and a tall bottle of water at his desk.

Lunch comes at one o'clock. We go to a nearby restaurant, owned by a couple from the Middle East. It is a very simple place, and it serves what I would call authentic Middle Eastern food.

"Middle Eastern food is not healthy, but you can get away with anything as long as you use good portions," says Dadirow, after ordering half of a dish. "The trick is to eat only as much as you need without filling your belly with unnecessary fat."

I ignore him and order a full dish anyway. It was

Kabsa, a truly magnificent rice dish cooked in veggies and lamb! It was made the Jordanian way, too. Yum.

After lunch, we went back to the bank. Dadirow was doing a lot of supervising, overseeing stressed out tellers. The place was filled with customers needing their banking issues handled after the weekend.

By three Dadirow was back to snacking. This time he had mixed nuts, maybe a fistful of it. He was snacking while on a phone conference.

At the end of his workday Dadirow was really stressed out, as a transaction did not go so well. So, when we left at work almost six in the evening, it was only natural he wanted to go straight to his place.

He showered, made some tea, and we watched television for a while, looking at the news and weather. Then, around seven, we went to his yoga class, to which he goes on Mondays and Thursdays.

Mondays and Thursdays are also "Friends night," says Dadirow.

At the yoga studio, we met up with some of his closest friends. Three guys: one straight, two gay. The five of us look like a clan, mapping our mats next to each other. People are eyeing us because we seem to be louder than the rest of the people.

"It is fun sharing this time with them," says Dadirow, between stretches. "I'm really busy, as you could see today, but I still make time for my friends. They are truly the light of my life. I can't imagine where I would be without these three."

He is right about being busy. On Tuesdays, Wednesdays and Fridays Dadirow goes to school at night—to become a Physical Therapist.

"My way of saving the world," he jokes.

Around quarter past eight, after some strong poses, we leave yoga for some Chinese food. We had some really healthy looking food, which by the way was also very authentic, apparently.

"Asian cuisine is not unhealthy," said Dadirow, fiddling the chopsticks through barbecued chicken and steamed brown rice. "But even this, you must eat the right portion. And it is really important to drink lots of water with any food."

And so once more he ordered less than I ordered. Oh, well, but at least some of his friends were ordering full dishes too!

At nine, we stopped by at a gay bookstore, where he buys a book on how to find the boyfriend within.

"I heard good things about this book," he says, browsing through the book while we wait to check out. "And the author is *so* sexy."

Uh-huh.

Less than thirty minutes later we arrive at his place. We watch an episode of *Sex and the City*. We talk about the women in the series, and Dadirow and his friends agree they have more things in common with gay men than they do with women.

Before we know it, it is eleven. It is time for him to go to bed. His day is officially over.

As I walked back to my hotel, in the cool Minnesotan night, I was thinking about how much this man had survived. I realized HIV was the least on that list, although it was the thing I came to get to know him for. It reminded me that we choose however we choose to live our lives.

Dadirow is definitely choosing to live.

Washington

I have many e-friends, but none do I like as much as I like Diriye. He is the older brother I often wished I had, and I often wonder what it would be like to meet him, talk to him, sit with him and share a Somali tea with him.

You see, Diriye is a living history. He was born in Isiolo, in what is now Kenya, which was colonized by the British, and so were his parents and grandparents in various cities in that area like Wajer and Garissa.

His family went to Somalia in the 1960s, a country that had just gained its independence from Italy and Great Britain, because of "the heady optimism of a united peaceful Somali nation; the NFDers, Somalilanders and Ogadenis were all flooding to the new capital," he says.

Soon, he spent his days in Jowhar, in the Middle Shabelle region, attending a boarding school. The American missionary school started in Jamame, in the Jubba, and moved to Mahadey, in Shabelle, and then ended up in Jowhar, by the Italian sugarcane factory and the mango groves. There, Diriye discovered about his sexuality and began to identify as a man who sexually prefers other men.

"The military regime expelled the Amish," remembers Diriye. "They were expelled for the counter-revolutionary activity of refusing to adopt the newly written Somali in Latin."

So, it was time to head to Mogadishu, where everything was new and unexplored and the possibilities seemed to be endless—people from all over Somali territories living and working, and making their way in the metropolis.

"It was a magical moment, when we learned of spaghetti, *sariir*, *cusbo*, *ukun*—all manner of new words we never used," remembers Diriye, fondly. "Mogadishu was so big, it had a population of thirty thousand and a taxi from downtown to Hodan was fifty cents. The local restaurants celebrated the union with a special plate of federation, half pasta and half rice."

For many people, who were new to the Mogadishu area, the foods, which were influenced by the Arabs and Italians, as well as Indian and Portuguese, were often too foreign to them. However, the food became an adventurous journey for Diriye.

"The southern cuisine included *canbuulo*, made of roasted coffee beans and the lovely azuki beans," he says, remembering the popular dish. "There was also *moos* and *mufo*, the wonderful tandoori bread eaten with banana and sesame oil. How delicious when mixed with *maraq*, that amazing sauce."

Diriye remembers a southern Somalia that was very different from what it is these days. He remembers a Mogadishu in which powerful men were openly known to be gay, he talks about establishments that catered to the lesbian community without any troubles from the mainstream society, and he recalls a transgender community in Marka that seemed to be open.

"I looked up the world homosexual in my dad's law reference books and found its meaning," remembers Diriye, who has lived openly most of his life. "I have been out since 1978, and my family, coworkers, neighbors and friends know that I'm gay."

He has been lucky to be able to live in Europe and North America, and these experiences have helped him to slowly come out of his own shell, says Diriye.

"It was extremely difficult coming out in the 1970s, but I fell in love," remembers Diriye. "I had a relationship in London, with a Scottish man who was also a teenager. He was kind, and gentle in helping me gradually come out and meet others like me. I joined a youth group and marched in my first Pride march."

Today, Diriye lives in the Washington, D.C. area. He is connected to the younger generation, people like myself, who would have had no history without people like him. In the Internet group *Queer Somalis*, which I co-created, Diriye used to post messages that uplifted people and often questioned the conditioned thinking of the younger generation.

But don't think he has had an easy life.

"I belonged to the original Muslim Brotherhood contingent of the anti-dictatorship movement of the early 1970s," he says. "I served as a *muazzin*, calling people to prayer, of a local mosque. Most of those members were shot dead by the military regime of that time. Some of us were lucky to have escaped with our lives."

He has basically lived the Somali modern history, from our early encounters with nationalism to the complete fiasco of the religious fundamentalism of today. But he seems to have found peace.

"Today, I'm spiritual and don't belong to any organized religious movement.

Atlanta

On March 22, 2003 I attended and spoke at a candle-light vigil in Marietta, Georgia. It was to protest a verdict that freed a man who killed a bisexual Somali man.

The killer, an African-American named Roderiqus Reshad Reed, said he killed his victim, Somali-born Ahmed Dabarran, in 2001 because the later and his friend forced him to have sex with them. At the time of the murder Reed was aged 18 and Dabarran was aged 32.

The defense attorney argued that Ahmed met Roderiqus on a telephone "party" chat line, and that his client was told there would be a party where girls would be present. When they met Ahmed showed up with another man and the two took Roderiqus back to Ahmed's place where, according to the defense attorney, eventually the other man forced Roderiqus at gun point so that have Ahmed could perform oral sex on him.

Roderiqus took Dabarran's cell phone, car and identification and admitted in court to hitting Ahmed several times in the head.

The defense attorney argued that killing Ahmed was justified in order to escape from him. He also used Ahmed's bisexuality in order to paint him as someone who led a double life, arguing that he was even married, although Ahmed was married through arranged marriage and did not live with his wife.

According to the prosecutor, however, Ahmed was hit on the head for about fifteen times and the medical examiner had concluded it happened while Ahmed was sleeping, arguing that there couldn't have been any danger to the killer from a sleeping man.

The vigil was as much against the prosecutor as it was against the verdict, because LGBT organizers argued that the prosecutor did not feel comfortable defending a gay case.

"I've concluded that Ahmed was victimized three times," vigil coordinator Steve Koval said to the crowd. "Once by his brutal murder, a second time by the disgusting lies his murderer told at trial, which were uncritically repeated in the news. And finally by the justice system which he served so faithfully—specifically, the Cobb County D.A.'s Office."

The information supplied by the prosecutor did not help the jurors. As such, the jurors felt they had no choice but to let go the killer, as one juror eloquently pointed out that the State had not "dotted their I's and crossed their T's," as quoted by the *Marietta Daily Journal*.

The family of Roderiqus had described him as someone who "gave his life to Christ at an early age," according to a website they had set up asking people to donate to their son's legal defense. However, online arrest records show he was arrested several times since then including in 2005, 2007, 2009, 2010, and 2011—all on other charges.

Ahmed, according to his brother Faisal, was someone who had gone through a lot of challenges in order to make a life for himself. He left Somalia after the civil war, came to the United States, and put himself through Law School. He became a very good lawyer, and worked his way up to becoming an Assistant District Attorney at Fulton County.

His boss, Fulton District Attorney Paul Howard, said his office had set up the Ahmed Dabarran Award, which was to be presented annually to a member of the Fulton County District Attorney's office whose work ethic reflected Ahmed's kindness and enthusiasm.

In the end, even if his killer was freed, Ahmed Dabarran was remembered.

The Future

Back in 2000, when I wrote about the story of a gay Somali for *Huriyah*, a magazine with a focus on Islam and sexuality that we had just founded the same year, there was virtually nothing in the news that was good about queer Somalis. I would go on to write about queer Somalis in 2001 for *ARISE*, an African-American magazine that has since went out of print. In 2002, I wrote for *Behind the Mask* in South Africa. In 2003, I wrote for *afrol News*.

Still there was nothing else. It frustrated me because I knew there were stories in our community that merited telling. A few years later, however, things started to slowly change. Suddenly, more and more positive news was coming out about queer Somalis.

It all started with the 2007 news announcement of a London group setting up a website for gay Somalis. The website, which was UK-focused, was in the news and brought a lot of young people out of the shadows of thinking they were the only ones in the United Kingdom. Steve Leng covered the story for *PinkNews*.

In a November 27, 2007 opinion editorial to *UK Gay News*, Andrew Prince, the editor of *UKBlackOut*, came out as the person who developed the website. He recounted how he had seen a lot of homophobia in the Internet, about the website, some going as far as to threaten the lives of the people behind the website.

Then, in 2008 Amal Aden's book came out in Norway. Her book, entitled "Se oss!" ("Sees Us"), was critical of the Somali community in Norway and what she called the enabling social welfare system of the country. As an openly lesbian, her work has encountered a lot of controversy and one time had to be living in hiding.

Today, she is one of the well-respected people in the country (see "Oslo" in this book). The queer community, both Somali and non-Somali, have recognized her contribution to the conversation about sexuality in the communities.

In 2011, an article written by Nicholas Keung for the Toronto *Star* reported on the new face of gay activism in that city. One of the individuals included in that story was a Somali young man named Lali Mohamed, a 23-year-old student of Ryerson University, who grew up isolated thinking he was the only gay person in the Somali community.

Mohamed runs Deviant Productions, with two friends, and they use video to tell the stories of their communities, including events and news. He is a fashionable young man, who is also very politically aware.

A year later, at Doc Now, Abdi Osman's "Labeeb," a portrait on a trans woman named Sumaya, appeared. The project was a combination of video and photography, and was well received during its May to June exhibition.

Osman's work focuses on black masculinity and how that intersects with queer and Muslim identities. It is such an interesting body of work.

In 2013, Noor Ali's article for *Al-Jazeera*, ended up creating a conversation on LGBT Rights in the Somali community. It interviewed an openly gay taxi driver. The taxi driver, a 25-year-old named Said Elmi, made an impression on the readers as a self-loving gay man. Despite its sad appearance on the surface the article was well celebrated in the queer Somali community.

In that same year another self-loving gay Somali made it to the news. Diriye Osman's very queer book "Fairytales For Lost Children" was published. A review by *The Independent* called him courageous and original. The reviewer, Bernardine Evaristo, said that the book features sensual, erotic, explicit stories "about young gay Somalis whose identities are shaped as much by their sexualities as their cultural origins."

But it has not also been all good news. Sumaya Dalmar, who went by the name Sumaya Ysl, the young trans woman in Abdi Osman's project, was in the news once more on February 22, 2015 when she was found dead by the police.

According to the Toronto *Xtra*, the police made a statement two days later saying she was found unresponsive and pronounced dead at the scene; and that her death was not suspicious. This was in response to social media rumors that her death was homicide.

The community did not agree with that assessment, given the fact that there was an eye witness interviewed by *Xtra* that said he saw a young woman running from a man, and the witness further stating he had called the police.

"There are so many deaths of trans women in this city whose deaths have gone unsolved and that is because, institutionally, Toronto Police Services does not give a fuck," Lali Mohamed told *Xtra* couple of weeks later on March 6, during Sumaya's memorial. "And this is an example of that," he added.

In 2016 the world is seeing another queer Somali story in the pages of newspapers and on television sets. Nur Warsame, an imam in Australia, shared his story of coming out—making him the first imam to do so in that country. He says his mission is to give young gay people hope.

"There is light at the end of the tunnel," Warsame told SBS, a public television network, "It can be a long tunnel at times, but there is light at the end of the tunnel."

What I love about the queer Somalis in the news is that the game has changed. We are no longer just some victims on the sideline, waiting for others to come and save them. No matter where we are queer Somalis are fighting for our rights; even against western police who are not valuing our lives, or faith leaders who don't recognize ours.

That gives me hope.

The future is here.

Glossary

These are words that appear in this book and for which a definition was either needed or to be provided for easier use in the future.

abaar - Famine.

adhan - The call to prayer.

adoon - It can mean "servant" (as "Adoon Ilaahey" or "Servant of God") or "slave", which in Somalia used for Mushunguli people.

af maay maay - A major language in Somali countries, second to the mainstream "Af Maxaa Tiri."

af maxaa tiri - A mainstream language spoken in Somali countries.

al-itihaad - Islamist grassroots organization that later developed into a more violent terror organization.

al-shabaab - Terrorist organization which came out of Al-Itahaad.

araweelo - Historical queen in the Somali community, often suspected to have been a lesbian.

baasto - Somali pasta.

baati - Garment imported from Tanzania.

bakaara - The second largest market in Mogadishu.

booyaaso - Maid.

buraanbur - Women's poetry.

cambuulo - Dish composed of roasted coffee beans and the lovely azuki beans.

cusbo - Salt.

dirac - Colorful kaftans wore by Somali women.

faan kuulo - Swearing word in Italian.

gabay - Men's poetry.

garbisaar - A shawl wore with Dirac.

goorgarad - Under skirt wore with Dirac.

gudniin - Circumcision.

guntiino - A dress wore by wrapping it around the body and tying over one shoulder.

huriyah - A magazine for and by LGBT Muslims, which was active from 2000 to 2010.

istunka - Festival in which people fight with sticks, a mocking fight.

kabsa - A Middle Eastern dish made of rice mixed with meat.

kauthar - A historical personality believed to have been a gay Somali. He was the partner of the caliph.

koonfur - South, generally referring to southern Somalia.

kumar sanu - A popular playback singer in India.

labeeb - Term for trans individuals.

lagaroone - A derogatory term for gay or bisexual men, generally similar to the meaning of "Faggot".

macawis - Somali sarong wore by men and imported from Indonesia.

madhab - A school of thought in Sunni Islam, generally four of them are accepted to be mainstream.

métis - A term used in France for people of mixed background.

muazzin - A person who calls people to prayer. Generally from a minaret.

mushunguli - An ethnic group in Somali that is part of the Bantu people.

niikis - Dirty dancing, generally with shaking the butt.

nin-nin - A butch lesbian.

qamiis - Muslim male dress in Somalia.

qaniis - Gay male.

qaniisad - Gay female.

raaf - Deportation.

reer xamar - Ethnic group of Somali-Arab mix, generally more light-skinned than mainstream Somalis. Also, a person local to Mogadishu area.

salafi - Ultra-conservative orthodoxical movement within Sunni Islam.

samaanyo - Gift given to a Yibir person on behalf of a new born.

sariir - Modern beds.

shafi'ism - The madhab most followed by Sunni Muslims in Somalia.

shahid bazi - The practice of witnessing beauty, generally using youth.

shaitan - The Devil.

shoga - "Faggot" in Swahili.

shuko - Somali chador.

sijjui - A Somali from Kenya.

suhuur - Meal eaten before fasting.

tafseer - Interpretation of the Qur'an.

takia - Sufi place of worship.

taraab - Swahili music.

ukun - Eggs.

uranism - A 19th Century term for homosexuality.

waaq - A powerful pre-Islamic god in Somali communities.

wadaad - A religious person.

waqooyi - North, generally referring to northern Somalia.

xalwad - Somali halva, sweet.

xamar - Secondary name for Mogadishu, generally used by

Somali people and especially ones from that area.

xashiish - Somali drug, same as hashish.

xawaash - Spices.

xawala - remittance.

About the Author

Afdhere Jama was born and raised in Somalia. He is the author of the books ILLEGAL CITIZENS and QUEER JIHAD, both on LGBT Muslims around the world. He was the editor of *Huriyah*, the first magazine for and by LGBT Muslims between 2000 and 2010. He lives in the United States.